Cambridge Elements

Elements in Critical Issues in Teacher Education
edited by
Tony Loughland
University of New South Wales
Andy Gao
University of New South Wales
Hoa T. M. Nguyen
University of New South Wales

PROFESSIONAL SUPERVISION FOR PRINCIPALS

A Primer for Emerging Practice

Mary Ann Hunter
University of Tasmania

Geoff Broughton
Charles Sturt University

Shaftesbury Road, Cambridge CB2 8EA, United Kingdom

One Liberty Plaza, 20th Floor, New York, NY 10006, USA

477 Williamstown Road, Port Melbourne, VIC 3207, Australia

314–321, 3rd Floor, Plot 3, Splendor Forum, Jasola District Centre, New Delhi – 110025, India

103 Penang Road, #05–06/07, Visioncrest Commercial, Singapore 238467

Cambridge University Press is part of Cambridge University Press & Assessment, a department of the University of Cambridge.

We share the University's mission to contribute to society through the pursuit of education, learning and research at the highest international levels of excellence.

www.cambridge.org
Information on this title: www.cambridge.org/9781009548151

DOI: 10.1017/9781009430685

© Mary Ann Hunter and Geoff Broughton 2025

This publication is in copyright. Subject to statutory exception and to the provisions of relevant collective licensing agreements, no reproduction of any part may take place without the written permission of Cambridge University Press & Assessment.

When citing this work, please include a reference to the DOI 10.1017/9781009430685

First published 2025

A catalogue record for this publication is available from the British Library

ISBN 978-1-009-54815-1 Hardback
ISBN 978-1-009-43067-8 Paperback
ISSN 2755-1202 (online)
ISSN 2755-1199 (print)

Cambridge University Press & Assessment has no responsibility for the persistence or accuracy of URLs for external or third-party internet websites referred to in this publication and does not guarantee that any content on such websites is, or will remain, accurate or appropriate.

Professional Supervision for Principals

A Primer for Emerging Practice

Elements in Critical Issues in Teacher Education

DOI: 10.1017/9781009430685
First published online: January 2025

Mary Ann Hunter
University of Tasmania

Geoff Broughton
Charles Sturt University

Author for correspondence: Mary Ann Hunter, maryann.hunter@utas.edu.au

Abstract: School leaders work in increasingly complex systems. Alongside leading learning, they daily navigate the needs and expectations of educational departments, teachers, students, parents, society, and themselves. Leadership can therefore be a dynamic vocational calling, but studies show that principals' professional agency, career sustainability, and wellbeing are diminishing. This Element brings a fresh perspective to how educational leaders can be better served and supported by collaborative, co-agentic partnerships at this time. It makes the case for Professional Supervision, a practice commonplace in clinical and pastoral professions that offers facilitated, action-oriented attention to the interplay of role, 'soul', and context. As a practice-based primer, this Element reclaims supervision against outdated associations with performance management by drawing on interdisciplinary research and the authors' own experience as supervisor partners with principals. It proposes a new schema of Professional Supervision in education informed by curiosity, unlearning, resonance, and attunement in a rapidly changing world.

Keywords: professional supervision, educational leadership, reflective practice, educator wellbeing, unlearning

© Mary Ann Hunter and Geoff Broughton 2025

ISBNs: 9781009548151 (HB), 9781009430678 (PB), 9781009430685 (OC)
ISSNs: 2755-1202 (online), 2755-1199 (print)

Contents

1 Introduction   1

2 'Nice But Not Necessary': The Vexed Place of Reflective Practice in Education   6

3 Frameworks and Practices of Professional Supervision   20

4 CURA for Education Leaders: A Schema for Professional Supervision in Education   42

5 Closing   66

References   71

1 Introduction

School leadership is a complex and dynamic role. The daily interplay of sustaining vision and values while navigating multiple systemic needs requires a diverse ever-expanding portfolio of skills and dispositions. While many leaders thrive in this dynamism, underpinned by a passionate commitment to quality education and service, performance is often framed by institutional priorities for compliance, accountability, and improvement. Expectations on school leaders are high in this regard and continue to grow: from pressures to improve student results on nationally standardised tests, to fostering positive behaviour, to enacting the reform needed for futures-oriented education in a climate-ravaged world. Underlying the challenges of this role, principals additionally find themselves at the interface of one of the most critical educational dilemmas of our time: how to both lead and learn in uncertainty.

Within this contemporary context, principals' wellbeing is diminishing. Critically high rates of stress, violence, and career-impacting burnout continue to rise, and speak to the very real challenges for individuals, as well as to the future of the profession. How can school leaders not only be supported in the technicalities of their role, but to think well, lead well, and be well with enervating and evolving demands?

This question is not new, of course. There is an extensive body of education leadership literature that seeks to address it and, in countries like Australia, a plethora of executive support services in coaching, mentoring, and counselling available. These services play a vital role in developing principals' capacities to manage their workflow and the associated compliances of school leadership. But while the question is not new, the context and expectations of school leaders are. Their professional oversight and responsibilities are intensified and in flux. More so than ever before, principals are expected to be prepared for, and lead for, unknown futures; so much so that the tasks of evidencing standards, complying with policy, managing people, leading learning, and directing projects may soon feel like only the beginning of the principal's tasks and not their completion.

Leaders' experiences during the global COVID-19 pandemic provided a sense of what it means to lead with greater uncertainty and to try to sustain professional agency, without being fully in control. The expectations and urgency of school principal roles changed globally overnight and were continually intensified by ongoing uncertainty. How does one prepare for the unknown? What helps resource and sustain leadership in such contexts? Our attention here, however, is not on *what* these pressures are or could be into the future, but on the question of *how* leaders are supported to cultivate purpose and agency in their work as they face continuing change. How are they actively enabled to navigate the relational, systems-focused, and affective-oriented dance required to resource and sustain themselves and their school communities through the flows and tensions of the everyday, as well as in the wider remit of their educational leadership in a changing world?

Professional Supervision is an approach to reflective practice that is a respected standard, and even a mandatory requirement, across many clinical, social work, and pastoral professions in Australia, New Zealand, and the UK. It is based on facilitated dialogue (conversational or creative) between a supervisee or group of supervisees and an independent supervisor who importantly is *not* the supervisee's line manager. The term 'supervision' in the education sector is problematic because it often suggests line management supervision, which focuses on competency, compliance and performance. This contrasts with the type of Professional Supervision we practise and discuss here, which orients towards reflective learning, ethics and vocational wellbeing. We explain this important distinction further by demonstrating how Professional Supervision effectively fosters clarity, agency, confidence, and agility, especially in roles demanding high autonomy and leadership. What makes Professional Supervision distinctive from other means of support such as coaching, mentoring, or counselling in the education sector is that it purposefully shifts the reflective lens beyond the technocratic aspects of professional life (reporting, assessing, strategising, for example) to matters of relationality, purpose, ethics, and value. In so doing, Professional Supervision necessarily *interrupts* practice, rather than merely reports on, interprets, or judges it.

A skilled professional supervisor facilitates this interruption by assisting a supervisee to notice the habits and assumptions they may be bringing – or fostering – in the entanglements of professional life. Supervisors invite multiple lenses on situations, events, issues, or relationships to enable critical insights to emerge, all with an orientation towards deep learning and ethical action. As a reflective practice, Professional Supervision recognises that leadership (or any professional role) is a relational process of ever-becoming: leaders are already and always affecting and being affected by change – in individuals, systems, cultures, and environments. Professional Supervision is therefore a practical on-the-ground response to the challenges of both leading and being entangled in a school's dynamic flows. In the place, presence, practices, and purpose of Professional Supervision, we hope to show how principals can actively navigate the competing and conflicting demands of their context, their role and their 'soul' (or vocational calling). Perhaps the most important contribution of an emerging practice of Professional Supervision to quality education is to support school leaders to move beyond merely *doing reflection* to identify or chart change, to *being reflexive* in the questions of how and why.

This Elements text aims to contribute to the education sector's growing understanding of Professional Supervision. As a primer, we hope to convey the value of reflective practice in education, introduce you to existing approaches of Professional Supervision in other professional sectors, and offer a schema for understanding what Professional Supervision could offer leaders in education, in this case school principals. We, the authors, are deeply immersed in the work of supervising, being supervised, and educating new supervisors as we write. We therefore situate ourselves and our writing as practitioners first and foremost. Drawing on the contours of the Elements format, we aim to share the frameworks we use for readers' practical understanding of what Professional Supervision is, in addition to our own testing and reflecting on relevant paradigms for its practice in education. While empirical evidence on the impacts of Professional Supervision is just beginning to emerge in scholarly research, this primer seeks less to prove Professional Supervision's worth, than bring light to the values, conceptual frameworks, and contemporary practice issues that underpin it at this time. We offer this as participant-observers informed by literature on Professional Supervision in other sectors, and the ongoing evolution (and tensions) of integrating reflective practice more broadly in school-based cultures and professions. We view Professional Supervision as a mode of professional learning in and of itself: a pedagogy that invites *being reflexive* with systems-thinking and affect-informed enquiry that goes beyond the sector norm of *doing reflection*. Being reflexive means noticing and realising – with curiosity as a guide – our own thoughts, feelings, beliefs, and doings, and the entangled impacts and influences they have.

Professional Supervision, it must be said, has had a slow uptake in the school sector and there are a few reasons for this. Firstly, the term 'supervision' itself has negative connotations of judgemental managerial supervision and, for teachers, may remind them of rather less-than-agentic experiences of being supervised on practicums or for the purpose of performance management. The legacy of school inspection processes and validation exercises is that supervision is assumed to be a process of evaluation and promotion. While not dismissing the important role of managerial supervision and reporting, this is not what Professional Supervision is about. Secondly, we believe there are complicated tensions within the education sector, in Australia at least, that have eroded educators' sense of their own professional agency. The growing demands for reporting and compliance are hindering the core values and goals of teachers' and leaders' professionalism. In this primer, we consider these and other factors that have led to Professional Supervision being under-recognised and under-realised as a support mechanism for change, before turning to emergent findings about its processes and outcomes in pilot projects that are exploring its relevance and effectiveness in this field.

Professional Supervision for Principals is written for school leaders, systems leaders, educators, and researchers. It aims to:

- identify the role and inhibitors of reflective practice in the field of education;
- describe key frameworks and leading pioneers in Professional Supervision as it has developed in other professional fields; and
- introduce a conceptual schema for the integration of Professional Supervision in education.

In presenting the case for Professional Supervision in education, we anchor our writing in our lived experience of its practice. There is limited existing literature in education studies on the approach we advocate here, so it is important to acknowledge the limitations of our claims regarding Professional Supervision. It is not the panacea for the ills of contemporary schooling, nor is it the only way to support education leaders' wellbeing or performance at this time. We hope this publication not only provides an introduction, but also a clarion call to deepen and expand its further reach and research. For instance, later in this text we comment on the need to consider how Professional Supervision can be more explicitly attuned and resonant with culture and place. As non-Indigenous practitioners working within the colonising systems of school and tertiary education in Australia, we seek to learn from and with First Nations supervisor colleagues in this continuing enquiry. What do decolonising practices of Professional Supervision look like, for example, once supervisors begin questioning the implicit values and assumptions behind the very idea of 'dialogue' as a culturally inscribed construct?

This text, while unapologetically making the case for Professional Supervision, is by necessity partial, exploratory, and invitational, rather than conclusive. We are cognizant of the impact that our own values and blind spots bring to its writing. Geoff has practised, researched, and taught in pastoral supervision for many years. He brings a theological worldview, extensive church leadership experience, and a strong social justice lens to valuing the power of transformation that Professional Supervision brings across many sectors and contexts. As a queer educator, researcher, and facilitator experienced in education leadership herself, Mary Ann first engaged with Professional Supervision as a student of Geoff's. She now supervises educators of all levels, experiencing Professional Supervision's relational, disruptive and creative potential in cultivating agency to counter the disquiet of business-as-usual in a rapidly changing world. Together, we have enjoyed jousting on the possibilities for new frames of reference for Professional Supervision and have sought to practise humility and activate responsibility in re-imagining supervision practices ultimately for more collaborative, just and sustainable futures.

In Section 2, we consider the place of Professional Supervision in education. We identify the enablers and inhibitors of reflective practice in schools to date, with an understanding of the increasingly complex roles that educators and leaders now have. We place the idea of 'professional' under the spotlight with specific reference to school leadership, and draw attention to the distinctions between Professional Supervision, mentoring, and coaching. In doing so, we seek to reclaim and re-align the terminology 'Professional Supervision', making its definition clearly distinct from outdated associations with management supervision, surveillance, or monitoring. Drawing on a small but growing body of research and our own experience leading a pilot course in Professional Supervision for school principals, we consider the value of this work in navigating uncertainty and supporting leaders to develop confidence and clarity in taking wise action.

Section 3 turns to the theory that underpins Professional Supervision. Beginning with the core concept of reflexivity, the section surveys the clinical, social work and pastoral sectors' contributions to the practice of Professional Supervision. Here, we adopt the practical approach of a primer to describe and bring a critical practitioner's lens to what matters most in the extensive training literature. We close the section with reference to Geoff's experience in a group supervision with a school's senior executive team as a way to exemplify theory in practice.

In Section 4, we deepen and expand the possibilities of Professional Supervision in education by drawing attention to the value of curiosity, unlearning, resonance, and attunement as conditions for practice. We explore this as a proposed schema, identifying how these conditions can be found in the place, presence, practice, and purpose of Professional Supervision in schools. Here we integrate our lived experience with contemporary theorisation about futures learning and leading. In this culminating section, we offer insights into the practical ways we see Professional Supervision making a difference in how leaders, educators, and, ultimately, learners become more agentic and open to finding clarity and critical hope in times of change.

As mentioned, we write from a practice-based perspective, integrating and applying our understandings not only of Professional Supervision literature, but to research on neurobiology, philosophy and contemplative care, as well as in contemporary sociology and education theory. While we do not take a unified methodology to the writing of this text, we do engage auto-ethnographically and creatively as we integrate practical insights with broader conceptual and theoretical frameworks and imaginings. In doing so, we draw on our current recollections of past experiences, recounting specific moments and recreating conversations to highlight certain points or ideas. This is most evident in our use of vignettes in this Element. These vignettes are not formal case-studies but are creative amalgamations of people, places, and encounters in supervision. These are therefore true to life but are not attributable to identifiable individuals or contexts. They are used here in the spirit of creative illustrative points.

We acknowledge the many people we have learned with, taught, and supervised over our combined years of practice. We are grateful to our own supervisors, Bobby Moore (Geoff) and Noela Maletz (Mary Ann), and to our colleague and friend, Michael Anderson. His vision and energy for supporting school leaders has led to initiatives that are increasing the awareness and practice of Professional Supervision in education as a force for critical hope.

2 'Nice But Not Necessary': The Vexed Place of Reflective Practice in Education

In this section, we:

- consider the vexed place of reflective practice in today's schooling sector
- draw attention to cultures of compliance that have given rise to overtly performance-oriented agendas for *doing reflection*
- show how this contrasts with the intention and role of professional supervision as *being reflexive*
- identify supervision as professional learning and contrast it with other mechanisms for performance-management and wellbeing
- draw on emerging research and evaluation of early implementation initiatives

'But I need to let you know, I'm very solutions focused. I don't have time for fluff – I'm not the fluffy type. I wasn't convinced I got what I needed with coaching, but I'm willing to give this a go. Will this really be for me?'

I (Mary Ann) am on a car speaker phone with a regional public school principal, Lee.[1] We've managed to schedule a moment to talk about professional supervision. I'm hurtling down a highway, and she's similarly on the move – on foot across her school's playground. The weather's looking dodgy and she's concerned about the prospect of flood, again. The need to inform parents is front of mind, as is her noticing of the already sunken school driveway. She checks in with the groundsperson as we speak about emptying

---

[1] Lee is a fictional character, a creative amalgam of encounters and conversations in Mary Ann's recollections of supervisory experiences. Names and characteristics have been changed, events have been compressed, and dialogue has been recreated but not attributed to single persons. The purpose of the vignettes is to provide insights into actual practice.

the oval shed of sports equipment ... which, she sighs, is only newly purchased following last year's string of so-called 'once in 100 year' floods. Ironically, a year before that, bushfires had threatened the school for weeks. Half-way through the call, she happens to remark the school's Strategic Improvement Plan (a working document required for all NSW government schools and re-developed every four years) is due in two days.

Well, the focus will be on what you choose to bring. I won't be setting the agenda, you will. If it's a solution you're trying to tease out, then that's what we'll focus on. As a professional, you're the expert of your own practice. I won't have the answers, but I'll bring the skills of holding space for your enquiry, offering an outside eye, and nudging you with the kinds of questions that others around you may not be in a position to ask. Sometimes you might want to test or better understand an idea or your stance on something – I'll be there to support you widen your lens of understanding, and help consider blindspots or the effects on others. Sometimes, a session might simply be an opportunity to stop serving everyone else's needs for a bit and choose to resource yourself. Sometimes, we will play with the 'what is' and the 'what if' of your situation or issue to find better clarity of purpose. Some people call it making the 'familiar strange' ... just as your flooding oval may look right now.

She laughs. She's going to give it a go.

Lee's wariness to invest time in reflective practice may sound familiar. During our short conversation, it was evident Lee was navigating multiple demands on her attention and time. She was tasked with making wise action on the run, alongside the background mental chatter related to her State Department's reporting deadline and, of course, the immediate and existential threat of the bewildering weather that day. By operating so many bandwidths at once, it is unsurprising that principals like Lee struggle to prioritise time for reflection – a practice which is oft-times assumed to be passive and voluntary, in contrast to the multiple layers of urgency when on the job (Baxter, Southall, & Gardner, 2021). In an overt culture of compliance (Sahlberg, 2016; Garver, 2020), taking time to reflect can be difficult to justify. It can seem nice but not necessary.

Yet, taking time for reflective practice is, we argue, a professional responsibility for educators and education leaders. Reflection has long been valued in scholarship of the learning process itself: reflection is the means that learners both *sense* and *make sense* of new knowledge and experience. This take on learning has strong resonance with leaders' needs to be both analytical and pragmatic on the run. Brookfield describes these as traditions:

- an *analytical* tradition that values reflective practice as 'a process of thinking better ... to recognise logical fallacies, think laterally and detect weak rungs on a ladder of inference' to enable better decision-making; and
- a tradition of *pragmatism* that 'sees reflection primarily as the analysis of experience' ... that seeks out 'new information, new understandings of existing practices, and new perspectives, so that they [the practitioner] can identify their blindspots' and revise their assumptions.

(Adapted from Brookfield, 2016, p. 13, emphasis added)

Our principal, Lee, is continuously engaged in cycles of discernment, deeply rooted in these traditions, as she makes numerous professional decisions each day. Of course, education writers prior to Brookfield have attended to the value of reflection both in action and on action. Dewey (1925), for example, is famously quoted as saying, 'We do not learn from experience ... we learn from reflecting on experience'; and further, Meziro (1990) and Schön (1984) are oft-cited for their contributions to the ways that critical reflection in, on, and for action contribute to improved self-knowledge and professional insight.

Drawing on the theoretical underpinnings that situate reflection as learning, a recent interdisciplinary exploration on reflective practice in the fields of education and social work determined a set of eighteen characteristics that span these analytic and pragmatic approaches. These include reflective practice as: 'a deliberate and purposeful activity that requires allocated time and discipline'; a 'reframing/reconstructing/reconsidering [of] decisions, behaviour, actions, reactions, responses, feelings, interactions, relationships, events, experiences, [and] perspectives of both self and others'; a process not always as 'necessarily concerned with 'solving-a-problem'; and an experience that 'can often be unsettling/uncomfortable/challenging/confronting' (Ewing, Waugh, & Smith, 2022, p. 6–7). Moreover, in examining reflective practice across a spectrum of professional applications, Ewing, Waugh, and Smith highlight that, by necessity, reflective practice itself 'is different in style and character according to purpose' (2022, p. 6).

This multitude of characteristics and purposes of reflective practice points, in part, to the reason principals like Lee find the idea of Professional Supervision as nice but not necessary. For in the education sector, reflective practice is not clearly defined or valued and is mostly experienced as *doing reflection* on evidence or experience, rather than *being reflexive* with it. As found by Ewing, Waugh, and Smith (2022), and affirmed by our own encounters in the education sector, leaders often associate reflective practice with the purposes of giving feedback to others, assessing compliance with professional standards and objectives, or as a component of debriefing after a critical event. These assumptions about reflective practice derive from an analytic and somewhat rationalist tradition where ascertaining the what, how, and why is the instrumental means to determining 'where to next'. It is well suited to a technocratic view of school leadership – a view that is prominent in the current climate of accountability and standardisation in education (Holloway, 2021).

We argue, however, that the contemporary and complex demands on educators to navigate multiple systems at once while cultivating futures-focused curriculum and dispositions (Larsen et al., 2023) in sustainable ways, calls on leaders to *be reflexive*, not just *do reflection*. In other words, our contemporary context asks leaders to consider 'the often unexamined nature of that which may lie behind the formation of ideas and beliefs that may be deeply embodied' (Groundwater-Smith, 2022, p. 136). To be the change-agents that many educational leaders were initially drawn to the profession of teaching to be (Perryman & Calvert, 2020), means taking up a responsibility to engage with the personal, organisational, societal, ethical, and cultural ecologies at play in their professional world. To our minds, the truism that 'the future starts here' in schools – as learning communities of children and young people who are and will lead the future – make this need for reflexivity on the part of principals and educational leaders urgent and necessary.

From Doing to Being: Hyper-Accountability and Burn-Out

Frameworks for this more reflexive-oriented practice have been established in sectors such psychology, social work, therapy, and pastoral care for some time, under the name of Professional Supervision. In some sectors, regular Professional Supervision has become a condition for ongoing professional registration or employment. While *doing reflection* is required for accountability and the necessary upholding of standards in these helping professions (Carroll, 2014; Hawkins & McMahon, 2020), *being reflexive* is critical to sustaining agency and autonomy within roles that have a strong ethical imperative. Yet, we wonder, as do many of the principals we currently work with, whether entrenched cultures of compliance in schools, and society's low esteem and trust for teachers (Dadvand, 2022), have eroded faith in the professionalism of educators, as well as in educators' own beliefs and assumptions about their agency. For principals, their work both affects and is affected by organisational priorities, professional standards, policy procedures, and curriculum mandates, as well as expectations of multiple stakeholders, including learners, teachers, other systems leaders, parents, and society.

Recognition of this complex assemblage of practices and affects sheds light on why the role and growth of reflective practice in education has become vexed. For within the terrain of contemporary schooling, the purpose and limited time for reflection can easily default to a performativity focus on how to achieve outcomes and find the least complicated and most time-efficient way to do so. While coaching as reflective practice has become commonplace for school leaders, we are noticing an increasing disquiet, particularly among mid-career principals, about the limits to the executive, performance-management prerogative that characterises coaching and, by default, can overly individualise and instrumentalise the paths to achievement. Similarly, traditional approaches to mentoring can be effective in cases whereby sharing advice about known or previously experienced aspects of the role can provide critical support. But this again can fall short of the kinds of assumption-challenging processes that a more explicitly reflexive approach invites. As Thompson (2022) notes, reflection without reflexivity can have the impact of driving effort towards evidence-building rather than towards thinking deeply about the professional role. To Thompson's point, we suggest that school principals, when navigating futures-focused leadership, are called upon to not only consider their professional role and purpose, but to recognise the growing necessity to think differently and creatively in these 'polarized, post-truth times' (Strom et al., 2018, p. 259).

While the benefits of educators engaging in instructional-style supervision have long been acknowledged (Zepeda, 2016), educators' degree of autonomy and agency in their everyday work can differ substantially from those in other helping professions in which Professional Supervision has become commonplace. Similar to the education sector, the nursing sector faced systemic tensions during the adoption of Professional Supervision. There were concerns that it might become a tool for surveillance rather than support (Northcott, 2000; Beddoe, 2010). Due to nurses' generally negative experiences with compliance and appraisal culture (vis-a-vis doing reflection for managerial supervision), the introduction of Professional Supervision to the sector was viewed with 'a flurry of interest, uncertainty and suspicion ... Was clinical supervision yet another attempt to control nurses?' (Northcott, 2000, p. 16). The wariness of nurse leaders at the time arose from perceptions of over-governmentality of the profession. Suspicions about Professional Supervision as an extra layer of organisational oversight and compliance thwarted the more optimistic views of its opportunity to engage with the need for *both* clinical feedback *and* critical reflexivity. The fear was that Professional Supervision, if implemented without due consideration of the systems in which it was to operate, was at risk of 'becoming another technology of surveillance and ... an opportunity to shape the practitioner into organisationally preferred ways of practice, even whilst veiled as being in the practitioner's best interests' (Johns, 2001, p. 140).

While this might not directly align with the experience of teachers as yet, Beddoe (2010) raises important considerations about the framing of Professional

Supervision as surveillance or support. Regardless of how effective the interactive and interpersonal processes of Professional Supervision are as professional learning itself, how can we foster and respect the value of professional agency within organisational and systemic contexts that are constrained by economic pressures and dominated by accountability and performativity agendas?

In our supervisory practices to date, we are noticing similar initial concerns about the co-option of Professional Supervision in the education sector, operating as most schools do within larger organisational power structures. This suspicion, tethered to a current collective sense of a lack of agency among school educators, is reflected in the work of the Global Education Reform Movement (Sahlberg, 2016) which is attempting to challenge the 'global orthodoxy of standardisation, narrow curricula, low-risk pedagogies, managerialism and test-based accountability' that underpin the culture of contemporary schooling (Cunningham, 2019). School leaders often find themselves at the mercy of this orthodoxy, working within increasingly complex systems and changing demands. As Andrews and Munro (2018) observe:

> In an era of hyper-accountability for schools and teachers, locating a dimension of teacher work that is not subject to some form of surveillance, performance rating or judgement is problematic. Usually connected to some larger system or school-level process of improving … outcomes, these demands call into question the perceived value placed on professional agency and trust. (p.1)

Moreover, 'teachers' thinking and work is at risk of being reduced to applying 'interventions' and 'treatments' and extracting any risk of deviation from 'what works" (Andrews & Munro, 2018, p. 2).

More recently, following the urgencies and uncertainties of principalship during the global pandemic, Cary (2023) cites philosopher Gert Biesta in warning that:

> the rise of top-down prescription of both the content and the form of education has significantly diminished the opportunities for teachers to exert judgement – both individually and collectively – and has rather put them under a regime of constant measurement of educational 'outcomes'. (p. 209)

It is therefore unsurprising that in this contemporary context, rates of burnout and attrition of principals and teachers continue to rise. In *The Australian Principal Occupational Health, Safety and Wellbeing Survey (IPPE Report): 2022 Data* (See et al., 2023), completed by 2,500 principals annually since 2016, it was reported that one in two principals have serious mental health concerns and are at risk of stress and burnout; that 44 per cent experienced physical violence from students or families in the preceding year; and that the number of principals seeking to quit or retire early had tripled in twelve months.

While Professional Supervision is not the panacea, our experiences and observations point to the potential of this work to strengthen leaders' vocational commitment, voice, and agency within a professional learning context, so that it is not left to an individual's responsibility for maintaining one's own health and wellbeing. In this, the Principal Survey data shows how less than 10 per cent of educational leaders identify their Department or employer as a source of support for managing the stress and challenges of their work, compared to relying on their partners (76 per cent) and personal friends (67 per cent) as their primary means of support. This data speaks of the increasing risk placed on principals' personal relationships to bear the weight of work stress. We urge the use of this data to instead draw attention to the wider responsibilities – and significant opportunity – for schools and school systems to better address their leaders' wellbeing with trusted long-term professional supervisory relationships which could ultimately help stem the departure of knowledge, skills, and wisdom from the field.

Cultivating Professionalism: Developing Clarity beyond Compliance

The issue of professional agency in the education sector has been a persistent concern for many years. In a 1975 publication titled *Professional Supervision for Professional Teachers*, it was argued that supervision 'is a neglected art in need of revival' (Sergiovanni et al., 1975, p. 1). It was thought necessary to break the entrenched divisions among agendas of accountability, improvement, and innovation in schools and the resultant negative impact on teachers' agency and motivation. The call at the time was to employ Professional Supervision practice as a way to enact change, arguing that any meaningful change in education or education systems was reliant on teachers, for '[i]n the final analysis it is what the teacher decides to do day by day ... that really matters and this daily encounter needs to be the focus of change' (p. 6).

Almost fifty years later, an understanding of compromised teacher agency motivates our similar call for attending to the art of reflexive-oriented Professional Supervision. Importantly, this is a call for *professional*, not *managerial*, supervision, and this is where nomenclature matters: for the term 'professional' positions a supervisee as an agent of their professional practice. Reframing and reclaiming the term 'professional' in Professional Supervision assumes a respect and trust of practice-knowledge and associated competencies. It offers a counterpoint to the legacy of surveillance and inspection, without losing the important role of quality assurance and accountability of conduct in a professionally coded and regulated role. Using the term 'Professional Supervision' also enables the sector to learn from models of Professional Supervision that have been developed and nuanced over time in other clinical and pastoral care settings.

How then can professional knowledge be valued to the extent that teachers and principals feel that they have, and can exercise, professional agency? Here we return to the importance of being reflexive over simply doing reflection. Billett and Newton (2010) draw on a long line of reflective practice proponents to argue that professional and occupational knowledge is generated and informed by continual acts of reflection and reflexivity. This knowledge, they argue, is formed and reshaped as a result of immersion in practice and a reflective focus on those who are ultimately the beneficiaries of that practice: in our case, students or learners. The purpose of being reflexive then, is to enable and embody meaning-making, identity-forming, and order-producing in work activities (Nicolini, 2013), in the service of others. The mark of professionalism, as we suggest here, is the capacity and commitment to be reflexive as a foundation for meaning-making, and to find the clarity needed to take wise action as a result.

Baxter, Southall, and Gardner (2021) further argue for the ethical imperative for reflexivity in education. Educational leaders' proactive decision-making is not just in their best interests as individuals performing a role but needs to account for the people, policies, and paradigms that both affect and are affected by those decisions. The skills and dispositions required to make ethical calls in such dynamic, multi-systems work environments require more than an instrumental or technical rationality (Schön, 1984). Taking wise action requires the kind of thinking awareness (McNiff, 2013) of an action-researcher, integrated with a commitment of care for the people, places, and cultures served.

In discussing the role of Professional Supervision in nursing and social work, Beddoe (2010) gestures towards active learning as a hallmark of professional agency, whereby the 'ideal supervision process would create a safe environment for people to "discover their learning edge"' (p. 1286). The call is to avoid an instrumentalist tethering of supervision to compliance, and instead towards a process of orienting practice and searching for saliences (Kemmis, 2005). Central to both these understandings is a belief that effective reflective practice should be primarily 'a vehicle for developing curiosity' (Thompson, 2022, p. 55). Here, we invoke Flessner, Miller, Patrizio, and Horwitz's definition of professional agency as working 'beyond notions of empowerment to living spaces of thought, tension and discovery' (Flessner et al., 2012, p. 6). This, we propose, is one of the core opportunities and purposes for Professional Supervision in education: it is an invitation to cultivate agency through conversation in 'living spaces' that draw upon educators' agentic and 'adaptive expertise' (Zeichner, 2018, p. 29) to generate wise action and change.

What the Research Suggests

What do we know from the research literature about Professional Supervision in education? How has it been implemented in education contexts to date, and what does this tell us about how it might work best into the future?

Although there is a rich field of scholarship on reflective practice, including journals dedicated to its exploration, research on Professional Supervision in school contexts is nascent. As Bainbridge, Reid, and Del Negro (2022) note, research on 'supervision in education [to date] has an instrumental and therefore performative, directional focus' and its measure of effectiveness has centred on 'the impact on standardised professional practice' (p. 547). Internationally, research with school educators point to conjecture about supervision's definition (Cornforth & Claiborne, 2008), and many variations of purpose and practice are referenced. For instance, supervision in schools in the United States is described as 'instructional' supervision and relates mostly to a practice of 'instructional leadership' (Glanz, 2022). Other supervisory research focuses on in-class supervision of pre-service educators (Bates & Burbank, 2019).

More recently, there has been a growing resonance between what we describe and practise as Professional Supervision (informed by the texts of Carroll, 2014, and Hawkins & McMahon, 2020), and explorations in education coaching (Andrews & Munro, 2018), futures-focused mentoring (Larsen et al., 2023), and teacher visioning (Vaughn et al., 2021). While the cross-pollination among these areas of practice offers a rich seam for further enquiry, here we cite a small number of evaluated practice-based projects that align most closely with the definition of Professional Supervision as we've experienced it in Australian settings. In addition to this, we report on the commissioned evaluation of a pilot course in Professional Supervision for principals that we recently co-facilitated in Sydney, Australia.

In a small-scale study in the UK, seven school-based Special Education Needs Coordinators (SENCOs) participated in twelve professional supervisions over a period of two years. Using Hawkins and Shohet's (2006) schema for Professional Supervision – focusing on supervision's developmental, qualitative and resourcing functions – the researchers sought the supervisees' feedback and insights as they engaged in 'working alliances' with trained supervisors (Reid & Soan, 2018, p. 64). The findings related to both the process and the impact of supervisory practice with these education leaders, with participants self-reporting that they felt re-energised in their work and that their professional resilience had improved. They perceived the impact of supervision as helping them avoid burnout, manage stress, and realise their vocational values (Reid & Soan, 2018). The researchers also observed participants' increased capacity over the life of the project to find their own solutions to issues and problems raised. The participants conveyed that they felt better at strategic thinking and believed that the supervision experience had enhanced their leadership development. In terms of the process, the participants felt that professional safety was vital to the effectiveness of the supervision, describing this as the provision of confidential and 'safe space' in a non-judgemental environment. It was reported that the supervision process' effectiveness was also a result of it being conducted outside the managerial gaze of the participants' schools' governmental authority.

Bainbridge, Reid, and Del Negro (2022) extended this small UK study to a further phase, conducting in-depth interviews with four of the original participants. Here, the researchers took a wider theoretical lens to the findings, referring to the 'contested nature of supervision in education settings' (p. 547), and explicitly commenting on the manifestations of a culture of governmentality in teachers' 'self-disciplining practice' (p. 548). The researchers found synergy between the aims of Professional Supervision and Biesta's concept of 'pedagogies of interruption' (p. 547). Their findings on the benefits of Professional Supervision were summarised as:

- *Professional learning*:
  - Enhanced critical reflection and processing complex thoughts
  - Better strategic management and delegation
  - Encouraging autonomy
  - Listening to and anticipating staff needs

- *Health and well-being:*
  - Reduced stress and anxiety
  - Better work/life balance
  - Improved ability to care for oneself.

(Adapted from Bainbridge, Reid, & Del Negro, 2022)

The research also suggested that the school cultures of some participants had shifted, with the case study of one of the participants, a principal of ten years, identifying that the time given to organise his thoughts during supervision had made him more aware of the importance for him and his staff to take more time to make decisions (p. 553). The researchers saw this as enabling a reconnection with the teachers' 'understanding of the purpose of education', such that 'headteachers can think and speak without judgement, therefore encounter[ing] … ideas beyond established practice and discourse to imagine and offer solutions particular to their settings' (p. 555). Here again, Bainbridge, Reid, and Del Negro refer to Biesta's call for educators' orientation to 'virtuosity', whereby a 'risky and open dialogue [can be] entered into, enabling the educational leader to make 'concrete situated judgements about what is educationally desirable' (Bainbridge, Reid, & Del Negro, 2022, p. 555, citing Biesta, 2012).

In another evaluation project, Elliot and Hollingsworth (2020) similarly invoke Biesta's concept of agentic virtuosity in reporting on the impact of the Menzies School Leader Fellowship Program which focused on cultivating leaders' capacity to build collective efficacy with others. While not referring to Professional Supervision by name, the project is worthwhile mentioning as it relied on participants engaging in reflective practice that sought to help disassemble the 'shady façade of the autonomous individual leader' (Bainbridge, Reid, & Del Negro, 2022, p. 547). This approach aligns with Professional Supervision's central concern with the 'unseen others' impacted by a professional's practice and reflects purposeful multi-lensed and systems-thinking approaches to facilitated leadership support. Biesta and Tedder's distinction between *eco*logical and *ego*logical thinking is referred to here, whereby *eco* refers to the agentic and co-agentic impulse across systems and processes, as distinct from the primarily autonomous and individualised *ego*centric approach to thinking and leading (Biesta & Tedder, 2007). As Elliot and Hollingsworth's evaluation of the Menzies' programme attests,

> Efficacy involves more than thinking positively or being optimistic. It is not a generalised trait, but rather it encompasses a diverse set of movable beliefs, tied to action and agency, which constitutes the ability to make things happen (p. 33, citing Bandura, 2012).

In this project, the relationship between reflective practice and efficacy to 'make things happen' was shown to be strong.

A Pilot in Professional Supervision Learning with Principals

The empirical and theoretical findings of the aforementioned studies are consistent with our own experience as co-facilitators of, and supervisors for, a pilot course in Professional Supervision for public school principals and principal coaches in New South Wales (NSW), Australia. This was initiated as a response to the developing crisis of principalship in Australia: with principals experiencing burnout, significant mental health issues, and violence leading to many leaving the profession (See et al., 2023). This course was introduced as an opportunity for principals to not only learn about reflective supervision and how to lead it with others, but to also experience it as supervisees themselves. Drawing on Geoff's decade of experience in supervision and training across various disciplines, and Mary Ann's background in educational and creative leadership, mentoring, and research, the course was tailored specifically for the education sector. The sixteen school principals and principal support workers (such as coaches and systems leaders) involved in the pilot were invited to engage in ongoing conversation and feedback as to the relevance of this application of Professional Supervision to their work as principals. The course was evaluated by Paul Kidson, a former principal and the co-investigator of the annual *Australian Principal Occupational Health, Safety and Wellbeing Survey*. Over four months, the participants engaged in eight days of practical intensives in addition to twenty 'clinical' hours of giving and receiving supervision, and submitted six written assignments ranging from reflections on their own supervisory practice to an essay on ethics. This enabled them to meet the minimum requirements for registration as associate supervisors with the cross-disciplinary professional body, the Australasian Association of Supervision.

Although the scope of the course evaluation did not include researching or validating the claims of supervision's impact itself, participants expressed that they perceived supervision as a valuable and essential practice for supporting principals' professionalism and wellbeing. Kidson's (2023) interim report determined that:

> Reflective supervision is seen [by the participants] as a more sophisticated and effective process than coaching and mentoring; it is much better suited to the nature of the transformational work required by contemporary educational leaders. (p. 1)

Participants expressed deep appreciation for the opportunity to reflect on the more 'spiritual' aspects of educational leadership, noting that this is rarely addressed in public education-endorsed professional development. They valued Professional Supervision for allowing them to consider the vocational, ethical, and motivational dimensions of being an educational leader, which are often overlooked in other support mechanisms. 'Given the challenging work of educational leaders, there is deep appreciation that the course addressed existential and spiritual elements of their lives' (Kidson, 2023, p. 1).

It was reported that the course's focus on Professional Supervision had 'changed some participants significantly'. In his final report, Kidson found that 'some, who started as "disillusioned with the system", have transformed themselves and now articulate their renewed desire to lead wider change' (2024, p. 5). While it's important to differentiate the impacts of the course experience from the broader claims about Professional Supervision, it's worth noting that the experiential learning programme provided significant insights into the overall value of professional supervision as a practice.

> Overwhelmingly, participants rated the program as one of the best professional learning experiences they had encountered. The emphasis on trust, relationships, 'seeing the big picture', and having freedom to use the language of 'soul' was refreshing. It was noted that, despite 'spiritual' being language in both the

Alice Springs (Mparntwe) Declaration and the NSW Department Wellbeing Framework, participants reflected this was the first time they felt it present and respected in professional learning for educational leaders.

(Kidson, 2024, p. 7)

These remarks on the course's relevance and effectiveness highlight what we believe to be the unique value and potential for Professional Supervision in the education sector. The role of principal often involves instrumental and performative practices that are largely and increasingly tied to regulatory frameworks for planning, measuring, and assessing student and staff achievements. However, Professional Supervision recognises the human spirit and its abilities for reflexivity, creativity, and ethical maturity in this. Ultimately, this is a relational profession focused on people and their capacities to learn.

Inhibitors and Enablers of Professional Supervision in Education

Many of the principals we work with find it somewhat ironic that, for many of the allied professionals who work in their school environments (social workers, psychologists, chaplains, pastoral care workers), Professional Supervision is commonplace. Yet, teachers and school leaders often are the first-responders to the personal, social, and systemic crises in a school, and the associated complexities that arise. Principals and teachers affect, and are affected by, the ethical and relational dynamism of school life and are always already entangled in multiple systems at once as they provide learning guidance and duty of care for others. The demands on teachers and principals to report, evidence, assess, and comply are increasing, without reflexive recourse to what is at stake for them professionally and personally when trying to access their agency in a world of complexities. Early research and our experiences in Professional Supervision indicate that having professionally facilitated spaces to clarify purpose, roles, and actions is crucial for sustainably navigating complex, multi-systemic environments. Although principals naturally strive to serve others and lead with conviction, there is minimal support or resources for these vital aspects, often referred to as the 'soul' of their work. Evidence is mounting that the costs are becoming too high for many principals to continue business-as-usual in their leadership. Climbing rates of stress, conflict, violence towards them, and burnout are making schools increasingly harmful and risky places to be, for leaders and learners alike.

In this section, we've argued that the increasing hyper-accountability agenda in schools has diminished the role of reflective practice for leaders. While leaders may engage in *doing reflection*, they rarely have the supported opportunity to *be reflexive*. We advocate for support processes that enable this reflexivity by reconnecting school leaders with a more agentic and sustainable sense of their core purpose. These processes should also recognise and nurture the conviction that initially drew many leaders to the teaching profession – to be change-agents in young people's learning lives.

From our experience, the practice of Professional Supervision, which acknowledges the interplay of 'soul', role, and context (Paterson, 2019), provides a confidential space and generative processes to explore the systemic and ethical entanglements of principals' working lives. Emerging research findings and evaluations of these initiatives in educational settings in Australia and internationally confirm their positive impact on wellbeing.

The Offer of Professional Supervision

While the term 'supervision' might evoke outdated inspection methods and the risk of being associated with surveillance and compliance cultures, Professional Supervision offers significant benefits to the school sector. Just as it has in other professions dealing with complex relational and systemically regulated tasks, it can greatly support the work of principals and educators. The development of Professional Supervision in the settings of clinical and pastoral care, as documented and theorised since the 1980s, suggests that it generates most impact when approached as a professional *co-learning endeavour* and when its purpose is for the supervisor and supervisee to *be reflexive* rather than *do reflection*. The kind of supervisory practice we discuss here brings explorative, agentic adult learning precepts to the fore, and acknowledges that the richest and most relevant outcomes can arise from contextualised reflexivity in and of action.

Although we focus on the impact for school leaders here, the potential remains for multiple purposes and impacts across the entire education sector. Research with supervisees internationally is showing promising findings, and we as 'pracademics' (Campbell, Hollweck, & Netolicky, 2023) seek to identify in our own approaches, the conceptual frameworks that are emerging for us, as we further discuss in Section 4.

Thus, the case for Professional Supervision in education is growing, yet still speculative. We bring our lived observation that supervision can cultivate educators' sense of agency by enabling self-determining professional growth in a supportive alliance that builds relationality, autonomy, and competence (Ryan & Deci, 2017; Bates & Burbank, 2019). We believe leaders and educators have a responsibility to be reflexive, and to cultivate reflexivity among others, as a core competence for society's necessary 'reworlding' (Chrulew & De Vos, 2019) in times of change. It is a practice that can be used to support systems thinking, critical reflection, and trustworthiness in the speculative and imaginary. In the future we are facing and creating, educational leaders' agency and co-agency with others is critical to the task of visioning a practical and potentially pluriversal politics of the possible (Escobar, 2020). We suggest that in this, quality Professional Supervision has a distinctive role to play.

In the next section, we bring the speculative to the realm of the possible and practical, by focusing on the *how* of Professional Supervision. We explore key practice frameworks and show how existing models and processes generate dialogic opportunities to engage safely with uncertainty (Mason, 2022) and cultivate a thinking awareness (McNiff, 2013). In outlining Professional Supervision as a pedagogy of and for change, we consider the practical applications of Beddoe's call to create the ideal supervision process as 'a safe environment for people to "discover their learning edge", build competence and utilise the energy generated by excitement and challenges in practice' (Beddoe, 2010, p. 1286).

3 Frameworks and Practices of Professional Supervision

In this section, we:

- further extend the focus of Professional Supervision as *being reflexive* beyond *doing reflection*
- identify significant conceptual frameworks and practices of Professional Supervision
- examine the key contributions of key proponents and writers in various disciplines and practice contexts
- consider a vignette example of group supervision in practice

We open and close this section with real-world supervision experiences. Some readers may be keen to skip ahead to the frameworks that follow, then return to this opening story. This is invited, as the writing of this section is the fruit of an iterative process of thinking with supervision theory and practice. It is our way of introducing a key approach to Professional Supervision called the Seven-Eyed Model devised by Peter Hawkins (1985) and detailed in a key influential text for cross disciplinary supervisor training, *Supervision in the Helping Professions* (Hawkins & McMahon, 2020). Within these vignettes, we capture a short precis of Professional Supervision's history and key tenants. Following this, we return to a central theme of this text: Professional Supervision's capacity to support participants to be reflexive rather do reflection. We do so by drawing on recent scholarship on 'thinking about thinking', and bringing attention to supervision's expanded focus on exploring questions of purpose and belief in professional life. In the third part of the section, we turn to the work of significant Professional Supervision proponents and their contribution to the developing conceptual frameworks and practices in clinical and pastoral settings: Michael Carroll (with Maria Gilbert), Joyce Scaife, Daphne Hewson, and Neil Millar. Bringing together this collection of contributions shows how supervision has developed beyond instrumentalism and a critique of practice, towards its value as a process of learning. These contributions have led to more recent understandings in today's practice of Professional Supervision: that it can be imaginal and ontological, not merely technocratic in approach.

Finally, we comment on the ways in which contemporary practice has been shaped by broader academic disciplines and discourses: for example, in clinical supervision where presence and partnering has been critical; in social work where advocacy and agency are key; and, in pastoral supervision which priorities vision and vocation. Here, I (Geoff) am indebted to two colleagues at the Institute for Pastoral Supervision and Reflective Practice: Institute director and writer, Michael Paterson, and my own supervisor for many years, Bobby Moore, a leading exponent of cross disciplinary supervision. Their writing – and the work of the Institute – has been an indispensable resource for the emerging practice of supervision in Australia.

An Emerging Model for Critical Reflexive Conversations

I (Geoff) am meeting with the senior leaders of an independent school, on the morning of one of their internal leadership conferences. The group comprises the principal, senior deputy principal, three other deputy principals, the chief operations officer, and the chief of staff. To begin, I provide a brief overview of the Process Framework for reflexive conversations. Following Bobby Moore's approach, I suggest to the assembled group that each participant would need three key resources to bring to our supervisory conversations: their emotional, theoretical, and practical intelligence. Short guided reflections lasting only 60–90 seconds follow as a way to prepare and help establish a hospitable space. Each participant is asked to pay attention firstly to their breathing and then to their body. Participants are invited to make any adjustments to their seating, the room temperature, the lighting, and so forth before continuing. Several turn off their phones, one asks for the lighting to be lowered, and one changes chairs. The group is now attuned to their own breath, bodies, each other, and the environment, and are ready for the next step.

The group are invited to share their hopes over two horizons. The first is the immediate horizon: their after-lunch session when another twenty school colleagues will join them. What is their intention for the next three and a half hours together before this happens? The second horizon is our last scheduled meeting for the end of the year. What is their intention for our work together over the next ten months? As each participant shares their hopes and intentions it is apparent that emotional, theoretical, and practical intelligence is gently and generously offered. They together bring a clarity of purpose to our time together, and we now have a group working agreement. As facilitator I am confident this group has the resources of the three intelligences necessary for our work together.

This first session continues with an exploration of the process framework utilising Moore's three rubrics: *reflexive awareness*, *critical reflexivity*, and *practical reflexivity*. A single page summary of the process framework is given to the participants which evokes a simple question from one of the new participants that proves to be a pivotal moment. The question is for a definition of reflexivity.

Fortunately, I catch my own reflexive response before launching into a definition. I am aware of my desire for two new participants to like and trust me. If I am able to provide a clear definition of reflexivity from the supervision literature my academic skills will be on display. But can I remember one? More significantly, is quoting a definition the most important thing to say? I share, instead, my own hesitation and uncertainty. Can I remember a good definition? Will that help? I notice my assumption (intuition) that I want to be an expert facilitator by providing good, academically rigorous answers. Attending to that assumption – bringing it to mind in the here-and-now – I make it available for collective critical reflection and deeper examination. My transparency regarding my own reflexive response demonstrates reflexivity, rather than merely defines it. In the discussion that follows, I feel it is a good call. In the words of Moore, the level to which supervisees will trust supervisors is directly related to how 'they experience the supervisors' credibility, reliability, and intimacy as collectively exceeding their self-interest' (Moore, 2017, p. 36).

I apply a further aspect of the process framework to this – given it is a group supervision and noting that the primary role is relational – and seek to cultivate an 'open heart and mind for empathic resonance' where the 'focus [is] on the emotional narrative' (Moore, 2017, p. 112). The process framework insists that emotional intelligence – characterised by vulnerability, empathy, and trust – is our starting point, not our end point, for the group's work.

I introduce the group to Nancy Kline's framework for 'listening to ignite', prior to beginning our group conversations. Kline states,

> The quality of everything we do depends on the quality of the thinking we do first. The quality of our thinking depends on the way we treat each other while we are thinking. The ten behaviours or conditions that generate the best kind

of thinking are: Attention, Equality, Ease, Appreciation, Encouragement, Information, Feelings, Diversity, Incisive Questions, Place.
(Kline, 1999, p. 17, 35)

By considering Kline's words, the assembled group of senior school leaders is beginning their supervisory journey with reflexivity by considering together the kind of thinking, listening and conversation needed. Perhaps this captures what we mean when we say 'thinking about thinking', and what Dan Siegel has in mind when he uses the phrase, 'reflective intelligence'.

From *Doing Reflection* to *Being Reflexive*: Thinking about Thinking

In many contemporary workplaces, professional leadership requires adaptability and agility (Heifetz, Grashow, & Linsky, 2009). There is a growing body of literature, confirmed by the lived experience of many school leaders we work with, that older, less flexible leadership styles are no longer suited to contemporary contexts (Kaldor, Nash, & Paterson, 2017). Recent developments in 'thinking about thinking' alert us to the value of being reflexive in such contexts and in the wider social environment of uncertainty and change. Research advances in neuroscience appear to confirm some and challenge other widely held assumptions about how we think. In certain instances, these discoveries have highlighted and examined our use of commonplace phrases such as 'trusting your instincts' (Polanyi, 2009); 'I need some time to think' (Kline, 1999); 'that was quick thinking' (Kahneman, 2011); and, 'think again' (Grant, 2021). Similarly, other writers have alluded to the importance of reflective practice in contemporary working life by referring to the mindful brain (Siegel, 2007) or the organised mind (Levitin, 2014). In this section, we consider the implications that flow from these insights to support our exploration of quality Professional Supervision as a process for harnessing thinking, encouraging reflexivity, and choosing considered wise action.

Gut Instincts: Friend or Foe?

More than generation ago, philosopher Michael Polanyi asserted that most people 'can know more than they can tell' (Polanyi, 2009, p. 4). In a landmark book titled *The Tacit Dimension*, he calls our gut instincts 'tacit knowing'. Many experienced professionals and leaders learn to trust their instincts over time. Yet, honest professionals and leaders will also admit they don't always get it right. Herein lies a paradox for instinctive thinking, decision-making, and practice: how can you know the difference? More recent research by psychologist Daniel

Kahneman reveals the question is quite complex. The more experienced the practitioner, the more likely they are to believe their instincts are right, even when substantial evidence shows they are wrong. Kahneman's conclusion is sobering for those who prefer to rely on their instincts:

> the confidence that people have in their intuitions is not a reliable guide to their validity. In other words, do not trust anyone – including yourself – to tell you how much you should trust their judgment ... If subjective confidence is not to be trusted, how can we evaluate the probable validity of an intuitive judgment? When do judgments reflect true expertise? When do they display an illusion of validity? (Kahneman, 2011, pp. 239–40)

In recognising this tendency in ourselves as well as in the school leaders we supervise, we notice the ways that Professional Supervision provides frameworks to discern whether gut instincts are friend or foe. Moore's process framework for supervision, for instance, invites a multi-lens approach that includes a focus on the absent or unseen other (Moore, 2010). In the case of Professional Supervision with school principals, this means bringing light to nuanced impacts on students, parents, or colleagues for situations or actions when they might not initially be the main focus of attention. The value of guided conversation using multiple lenses for reflection is further highlighted by Kahneman's distinction between thinking fast and slow.

Fast and Slow Thinking: Is Quick Thinking a Virtue or Vice?

Quick thinking and gut instincts are related but not identical facets of thought and decision-making. Kahneman distinguishes quick thinking as 'System 1' and slow thinking as 'System 2' whereby:

> System 1 operates automatically and quickly, with little or no effort and no sense of voluntary control. System 2 allocates attention to the effortful mental activities that demand it, including complex computations. The operations of System 2 are often associated with the subjective experience of agency, choice, and concentration (Kahneman, 2011, pp. 20–21).

Agency and choice. Attention and concentration. Complexity. These, according to Kahneman, exist in the realm of slow (not fast) thinking. Having provided Professional Supervision to senior leaders in church contexts, armed services, and now schools for over ten years, I (Geoff) am no longer surprised at just how critical it is to slow down the conversation (and thinking) in sessions, so leaders can regain their sense of agency and discover they have choices – not merely decisions – to make. The ability to think quickly, a trait of most senior leaders in time-pressured complex roles, must be considered a virtue but also, if unchecked, a vice that can potentially diminish agency, choice, attention, and concentration.

Time to Think: Listening to Ignite Thinking for Wise Practice

Nancy Kline makes explicit the link between the quality of thinking and listening in our relationships: 'the quality of everything we do depends on the quality of the thinking we do first. The quality of our thinking depends on the way we treat each other while we are thinking' (Kline, 1999, p. 17). Listening and thinking are therefore entwined as a relational act – evident in the purpose and context of Professional Supervision which seeks to ignite reflexivity and thinking in choices towards wise action. As noted previously, Kline suggests there are three types of listening: listening to interrupt, listening to understand, and listening to ignite (Kline, 1999). In a noisy and competitive environment, fuelled by the 24/7 media cycle, contemporary society is plagued by interruptions to listening, thinking, and reflecting. It is therefore unsurprising that school leaders, operating in large and complex ecosystems with busy, overcrowded timetables, often listen to interrupt with the intention to respond or fix quickly. It can become an efficiency default leading to an overall preferred way to interact. While quick thinking has its benefits in the more technocratic aspects of school management, curiosity, and reflexivity can often be displaced by time pressures and a culture of continual crisis management. As many of our school leader supervisees have confided, too few opportunities exist for taking a reflexive rather than reactive route to dealing with things that trouble them.

Thinking Again: Unlearning for Wise Practice

At the centre of organisational psychologist Adam Grant's thesis in *Think Again: The Power of Knowing What You Don't Know* is the simple idea, and incredibly difficult activity, of unlearning. While we consider unlearning as one of four core conditions of quality supervision in Section 4, it is important to note here that Grant stereotypes the leader who is unwilling to 'think again' (in effect, to unlearn) categorically as either a preacher, a prosecutor, or a politician. Leaders who refuse to unlearn become trapped in 'overconfidence cycles' whereby they 'form an opinion that feels right, seek information to support that opinion, feel validated and proudly express opinions' (Grant, 2021, pp. 3–4). While the preachers, prosecutors or politicians in our midst might feel unfairly maligned by Grant's characterisation (I, Geoff, was a preacher for a couple of decades), many leaders might squirm uncomfortably in recognition of Grant's claims. Busy schedules, constant interruptions, the pressures from various stakeholders with their competing, irreconcilable demands – no aspect of this environment supports the acts of thinking slow, taking time to think, or thinking again. In the context of education, neuroscientist Dan Siegel suggests that reflection should be the fourth R of education (Siegel, 2007), not only for students but, we argue, for educators and education leaders as well. For while doing reflection is expected in the case of assessing job performance or evidencing system standards or improvement plans, reflexivity as deep learning – 'thinking about thinking' to notice beliefs and biases that inform everyday thinking – should be critical across all aspects of contemporary school life.

Before returning to the vignette of Geoff's senior executive team in group supervision, it is worth acknowledging the broader themes from Siegel's research that relate to the underpinning quality of intention in Professional Supervision.

Deeper Thinking for Intention and Fidelity in Practice

In his discussion of the mindful brain, Siegel draws on the perspective of interpersonal neurobiology to acknowledge and embrace the wide array of ways to know: 'from the broad spectrum of scientific disciplines to the expressive arts and contemplative practice' (Siegel, 2007, p. xvii). Like many of the writers surveyed here, the importance of paying attention – 'focusing awareness on a very specific mental process: our own intentional state' – is crucial for Siegel:

> Intentions tie a given moment of life together, link actions now with actions of immediate next moment, creating the underlying 'glue' that directs attention, motivates action, and processes the nature of our actions.
> (Siegel, 2007, p. 178)

The implication for how effective school leaders could be supported to think well, lead well, and be well via *attention to their intentions* is significant here. As a kind of diagnostic for quality supervisory practice itself, we can draw on Siegel's identification of the seven functions of the middle prefrontal cortex that are associated with 'attending to intention': 'body regulation, attuned communication, emotional balance, response flexibility, empathy, self-knowing awareness, and fear modulation' (Siegel, 2007, p. 191).

We will return to Siegel's work in our discussion of attunement and resonance in Section 4. However, it is important here to recognise the ways in which Professional Supervision, as exemplified in our case of the school's executive team, invited attention to intention; and, in doing so, enabled participants to engage in processes of dialogue and embodied noticing that made the workings of these seven functions explicit.

Frameworks for Learning in Professional Supervision

While understandings of neuroscience strengthen the rationale for Professional Supervision, what are the conceptual frameworks for its practice? What underpins and distinguishes quality reflexive practice in supervision? What actually happens and why?

There are many accessible in-depth handbooks on Professional Supervision that explain its practice in detail and have guided its introduction and training in clinical and pastoral settings since the 1980s (Hewson & Carroll, 2016; Davys & Beddoe, 2020; Hawkins & McMahon, 2020). Rather than replicate the detail and intent of these texts, we turn to the work of those who have made significant contributions towards our own understandings of practice, relevant to supervision in the school sector. Here, we refer to *the what* of supervision through Michael Carroll's five point overview, before turning to Carroll and Maria Gilbert's categorisation of different levels of reflection, Moore's process framework, and finally to the Seven-Eyed Model (Hawkins, 2011; Hawkins & McMahon, 2020) as a predominant approach in contemporary practice.

Professional Supervision Is Learning through Reflection (Michael Carroll with Maria Gilbert)

Michael Carroll's five-point summary of Professional Supervision is one of the clearest expressions of *the what* of supervision:

1. The focus of supervision is practice.
2. The end result of supervision is learning (the deepest form of which is transformational learning).
3. The method used in supervision is reflection (reflection, reflexivity, critical reflection, and critical self-reflection).
4. Supervisors facilitate that process by creating an environment and relationship that mediate learning.
5. The supervisory relationship is the engine room.

(Carroll, 2014, p. 18)

Carroll's middle point here is key. We understand reflection as the method and we argue in the case of supervision in education that reflexivity is the most generative and the most needed in the current context of contemporary school leadership.

With Gilbert, Carroll later categorised six levels of reflection, from the disconnection of no reflection to the universal connections of a more transcendental stance (Carroll & Gilbert, 2011, p. 220). Before reviewing these levels and their applicability to Professional Supervision, it is worth noting that the levels are designed as incremental, developing from what Carroll calls a level of 'me-stance' reflection, through to reflection that embraces relationality with systems of greater complexity. The Seven-Eyed Model of Supervision (Hawkins, 2011; Hawkins & McMahon, 2020), as noted already, captures an activation of this relational and systemic approach, but does not preferentially categorise these 'eyes' (herein referred to as Modes) as similarly graduated. Rather, in the Seven-Eyed Model, the supervisory experience is like a *dance* among these modes as they focus variously on:

- the situation the supervisee brings and their strategies and interventions (Modes One and Two)
- the supervisee's relationship with others they serve (Mode Three)
- the supervisee themself (Mode Four)
- the supervisory relationship itself (Mode Five)
- the supervisor's own experiences (Mode Six)
- the wider contexts and systems in which the work happens (Mode Seven).

(Adapted from Hawkins & McMahon, 2020, p. 85)

It is important to note here, that these latter modes (Five, Six, and Seven), and the intentional integration of all modes can be described as characteristic of Professional Supervision, and has made it distinct in the past from conventional traditions of coaching and mentoring.

Professional Supervision therefore invites multiple modes of reflection that enable reflexivity: in other words, it gives rise to 'thinking about thinking' that draws attention to underlying beliefs, attitudes and assumptions, and can therefore engage with a more ethically mature and potentially transformative 'seeing beyond' (Carroll & Gilbert, 2011, p. 222). Carroll and Gilbert refer to this as 'what makes meaning and what gives meaning to life', thereby inviting 'higher or larger perspective(s) that help ... make sense of life and purpose' (Carroll & Gilbert, 2011, p. 222). Elsewhere, this meaning-making perspective is aligned with inner-life and 'soul' work. As a scholar-priest in a Judeo-Christian tradition, I (Geoff) have been pleasantly surprised that this spiritually inflected language has resonated strongly in Professional Supervision teaching with people of other faiths and no faith (Kidson, 2024); and I (Mary Ann), as a contemplative practitioner oriented by non-Christian traditions, have recognised supervisees' yearning to get to the 'real heart and soul' of matters intimating their resonance with bigger pictures of purpose in role and life, beyond simplified cause-and-effect or wholly anthropocentric ways of seeing-and-sensing. This more expansive level of reflection, Gilbert and Carroll note, 'transcends any particular relationship, person or situation, opening into a larger construct that is inherent in all relationships, people or situations' (Carroll & Gilbert, 2011, p. 222). Rather than making this attention abstract or arbitrary, the guided conversations of Professional Supervision invite supervisees 'to live [their] current situation through expanded perspective, and recognise [their] own personal limitations of perception.' Carroll and Gilbert describe it as the opportunity to 'expand my 'little self' and embody qualities ... that guide, teach and inspire me' (Carroll & Gilbert, 2011, p. 222).

At another end of the spectrum, reflection can often be dismissed as superficially or singularly navel-gazing. Professional Supervision inherently avoids this by consciously applying frameworks that require multiple modes and lenses of reflection. It is an affective and metacognitive dance of thinking, feeling, talking, and doing: a sensing as well as a making sense, a thinking about thinking, and an invitation to questions about what drives beliefs, values, biases, and blind spots. For example, 'How are the unseen others in this situation impacted?' In Carroll and Gilbert's description of the level of 'zero reflection', a supervisee may find it 'difficult to go internal, or to look at wider pictures or bigger systems' (Carroll & Gilbert 2011, p. 220). This lack of reflection – or rather, capacity for reflection – inevitably leads to a 'black-and-white stance to making sense of events and is based on a theory of causality and reporting that is very simplistic, such as "*this* caused *that* to happen"' (Carroll & Gilbert 2011, p. 220, emphasis added). Leaders who are unwilling to engage beyond this basic level of reflection might therefore characterise reflective practice as navel gazing if the connection to action is not made. Unfortunately, this can lead to a default shaming or blaming of others, because 'there is little consideration for how [they, the supervisee] might be part of the problem or contribute to it' (Carroll & Gilbert, 2011, p. 220).

Quality supervision enables the supervisee to slow down, pause, and reflect on practice for the purpose of taking wise action. For this to happen, Carroll and Gilbert describe the early stages of creating the supervisory alliance as empathic. With an observer stance, a supervisor can offer 'a more compassionate interpretation [that] allows for insights into what is happening to the other' (Carroll & Gilbert, 2011, p. 220). A collaborative and relational reflective stance can then be developed when personal connection is made, 'shared space' is cultivated, and the awareness that through dialogue 'we create a relational dilemma for which we both have some responsibility' (Carroll & Gilbert, 2011, p. 220).

The systems-perspective of the Seven-Eyed Model of supervision is, we believe, crucial to quality supervision in education. In addition to the benefit of offering multiple initial entry points into reflection and dialogue, its systemic reflective modes acknowledge the dynamics of the various systems and contexts that school leaders navigate, asking 'how is it all connected and how can we see and reflect from these multiple perspectives?' Supervisors often invoke the image of a helicopter (or satellite), as a way to describe the 'ability to see the various small and large systems that affect our lives and our behaviour' (Carroll & Gilbert, 2011, p. 221). The art of supervision is to realise that the bigger picture is not separated from the necessary internal self-reflection: systems influence and affect people, just as people influence and affect systems. Gilbert and Carrol observe that, when held together, the supervisee often realises, 'Gosh!, it's actually about me!', because insight on ways of working and meaning-making emerge from taking integrated perspectives.

Being reflexive, or taking a reflexive stance, captures this integration. It is the opportunity for a supervisee, in our case a school leader, to think systemically and relationally, while also 'thinking about their thinking'. In so doing, they are invited to see their part, their movement, their resonance in a bigger dynamic, a bigger whole. In the Seven-Eyed Model, this integrated perspective is critically explicit in Mode Five whereby, in the relationship between supervisor and supervisee, the reflection on the *there-and-then* enters the *here-and-now* (Hawkins & McMahon, 2020, p. 88).

Modes Six and Seven in the model weave together both the inner perspective (the reflexive stance of the supervisee) with the wider, systems perspective, aligning back to Gilbert and Carroll's highest levels of reflection:

> This is the reflective stance that sees 'beyond' to what makes meaning and what gives meaning to life. I am willing to adopt this expanded view/state of being, even though it may require me to enter a space of 'not knowing', and may engender a profound restructuring of my mental constructs.
>
> (Carroll & Gilbert, 2011, p. 222)

Carroll and Gilbert's significant contribution to our understanding of Professional Supervision is that it invites and engenders 'not knowing'. While Buddhist traditions refer to this as beginner's mind, educators have long known that all true learning begins at the edge of not knowing. Carroll has more recently articulated this as 'uncertainty': 'ask me what I do as a supervisor and I will reply that I have become a facilitator of reflection and that I manufacture uncertainty. It was allowing myself to be uncertain that first introduced me to reflection' (Hewson & Carroll, 2016, p. x). How, then, does learning through uncertainty and not-knowing shape supervisory practice? That is addressed in Joyce Scaife's approach to reflexivity in practice.

Professional Supervision Is a Relational Act, Cultivating Conditions for Reflexivity (Joyce Scaife)

> In the context of professional practice I understand the term reflexivity to describe any process that includes itself within its own imperative ... If, as a teacher or supervisor, I prevail upon students and supervisees to adopt a curious and

questioning attitude, and I exemplify this in my own teaching and supervisory practice then I am adopting a reflexive stance ... From a reflexive perspective we include ourselves in our thinking about our work because the accounts that we give cannot be independent of the observer. (Scaife, 2010, p. 8)

For Joyce Scaife, a supervisor, writer, and researcher in mental health supervision, keeping reflexivity in mind, 'allows me to check that an opportunity for congruence between my beliefs and my actions has not been missed' (Scaife, 2010, p. 9). The contribution of Scaife's work is the understanding that the Professional Supervision experience itself is a process of co-constructing meaning. This is present in questions such as 'How is this process going?' and 'How are we doing?' (Scaife, 2010, p. 9). Resonant with Brookfield (2016) and Schön (1984), Scaife identifies five challenges or obstacles to quality reflective practice in supervision. These include:

- persistence of traditional values,
- organisational culture,
- impossibility of standing outside context,
- fear of appearing incompetent, and
- fear of opening oneself to scrutiny and of emotional connectedness

(Scaife, 2010, p. 18).

Quality practice in Professional Supervision is therefore reliant on the development of trusting relationships whereby supervisors can hold and not judge supervisees' vulnerabilities. This is particularly important for leaders such as school principals who regularly say they 'just get on with it' and rarely acknowledge, let alone express feelings of vulnerability in the working day. The most effective kind of relationship in Professional Supervision to develop this trust, Scaife suggests, is one premised on 'strong supervisory alliance', whereby supervisees can reveal 'their insecurities, their successes, and their innermost thoughts and feelings in order to critically review how these are impacting on their work' (Scaife, 2010, p. 24).

In these ways, Scaife foregrounds Professional Supervision as a relational act: one of *walking with* supervisees as they draw on diverse ways of knowing themselves, others, and the contexts in which they work. Scaife describes these diverse ways of knowing as important and present (in varying degrees) in all supervisory encounters. They include:

- aesthetic ways of knowing: 'grasping, interpreting, envisioning what is to be achieved';
- personal ways of knowing: 'in terms of the practitioner's [supervisee's] own mental models, vision, attitudes, feelings, concerns and ignorance';

- ethical ways of knowing: 'what is judged to be the best or right action or non-action'; and
- empiric ways of knowing: 'what is accessible through the senses that can be observed and measured in some kind of way'

(Scaife, 2010, p. 31).

In the supervisory alliance, ideally the supervisor is alert to the diverse ways of knowing available to the supervisee's own reflexive process and is able to direct and facilitate attention to them and between them as needed.

So far, through the work of Paterson, Gilbert, and Scaife, we have described Professional Supervision as reflexive learning and as a relational act that draws on diverse ways of knowing. Next, we consider the key processes within the supervision encounter with Hewson and Carroll's framework of noticing, considering and consolidating, before again expanding our view to the types and functions of Professional Supervision as they are relevant to educational leadership.

Supervision Is a Process of Noticing, Considering, and Consolidating (Daphne Hewson with Michael Carroll)

I (Geoff) have been supervising and teaching professional supervision for more than decade, and one of the assessment tasks I regularly set is for students to search for, select, and precis an article on supervision theory that connects to their own practice. Often, the works of Carroll and Paterson come up. This is partly because of the volume of writing they have published, but also because of their ability to succinctly capture the heart of supervision in pithy, practical terms: for example, Paterson's description of supervision as noticing, wondering and realising (Leach & Paterson, 2015).

Similarly, Daphne Hewson and Carroll provide a summary of the supervisory process as 'noticing, considering and consolidating' (Hewson & Carroll, 2016, p. vi). They articulate how reflective practice within Professional Supervision comprises both reflection *on* practice and reflection *for* practice, arguing that Schön's concept of reflection *in* action (or practice) can be really difficult, even for the most practised professionals (Hewson & Carroll, 2016, p. 40). They instead distil the process of a supervisory session as: 'learning how to notice what's happening, learning how to analyse it and unpack the assumptions that underpin it, and learning how to put this into practice, so that it becomes routine' (Hewson & Carroll, 2016, p. vi).

Carroll's long experience as a leading theorist and practitioner of supervision has taught him two essential truths: 'supervision is first and foremost for supervisees' and 'supervision is primarily a reflective conversation' (Hewson

& Carroll, 2016, p. x). If supervision is primarily a reflective conversation, then 'it is with reflection-on-practice and reflection-for-practice that supervision finds its true home' (Hewson & Carroll, 2016, p. x). Noticing, considering and consolidating are key to this process, as they enable the entanglements of past, present, and future to ignite discussion. Carroll is fond of quoting Kierkegaard, 'you live life forwards, you understand it backwards' (Carroll, 2011, p. 15), such that supervision 'meditates on the past in the present to prepare the future' (Carroll, 2011, p. 27). Therefore, *noticing* involves 'pausing and noticing to become fully aware'; *considering* involves 'making sense of what you've noticed by careful exploration and analysis, particularly of the assumptions and values that underpin it'; and *consolidating* 'translates new learning into practice' (Hewson & Carroll, 2016, p. 41–45).

This scaffold for Profession Supervision offers a simple harness for conversations on the complexities of everyday professional life. In our experience, senior leaders across various professions often report that, once introduced to it through supervision, they utilise this same scaffold for other aspects of their own leadership and teaching and find it a useful way of bringing the there-and-then into the here-and-now to inform future action.

Professional Supervision Moves beyond the Instrumental and Critical, to the Imaginal and Ontological (Neil Millar)

In his recent doctoral studies, supervisor and researcher, Neil Millar, makes the case that Professional Supervision attends to matters beyond the instrumental and critical, towards the imaginal and ontological. In other words, Millar's work attests to the value of maintaining integrity in *being reflexive*, beyond the act of *doing reflection* as a means of compliance or evaluation. It is worth considering in more detail here what Millar means by these types of reflection, so the distinctive purpose and value of Professional Supervision compared with other professional support mechanisms for leaders can be realised.

Instrumental Reflection

Similar to the graduated levels of reflection described by Carroll, Millar refers to instrumental reflection as 'simple problem-solving', focusing on the 'nuts and bolts of past action and usually involves such things as reviewing, diagnosing, analysing, strategising and deciding' (Millar, 2018, p. 46). Many leaders, by necessity, must employ instrumental approaches to enable and enhance their team or organisation's effectiveness and efficiency. This is particularly true of leaders operating in complex systems like schools. Without instrumental reflection and accountability to standards, students and teachers would suffer the consequences of ineffectual practices or inefficient processes of education. Yet, narrowing all reflective practice in school leadership to a sole focus on instrumental reflection would generate only 'technical and behavioural knowledge – that is, knowledge to do with means and ends, with the what, when, where and how of action', rather than the critical or 'ethical dimensions of practice' (Millar, 2018, p. 46) – the why.

Instrumental reflection is usually management-driven and compliance-oriented and, as Millar suggests, is often rife when there is organisational restructuring, streamlining, and cost-cutting – thereby leaving little agency for reflection on values. Often, when consultants or coaches are employed by organisations to foster better and improved practices, compliance rather than fidelity becomes the goal. And while attending to matters of compliance may be one aspect of Professional Supervision's normative function, when instrumental reflection is disconnected from a consideration of values, ethics, and sense of deeper purpose, its capacities for genuine reflexivity and new insights are limited.

Critical Reflection

Teachers and school leaders will be familiar with the processes of critical reflection in their education studies. In theory and practice, critical reflection entwines two main emphases: the personal and cultural. Both require uncovering and evaluating the taken-for-granted assumptions, norms, beliefs, and embedded power relations that can constrain practice. Millar offers a compelling description of critical reflection as

> more difficult than instrumental reflection, not only because it calls on complex ways of thinking but also because the focus moves from external practical issues to the consideration of internal values and beliefs, as well as of broader historical, socio-political and cultural issues. [Yet] Critical reflection ... tends to privilege rational thinking over and against embodiment, emotion, transformative learning. (Millar, 2018, p. 49)

The importance of critical reflection within Professional Supervision is to engage with questions of power and the underlying effectiveness of their practice: what values or beliefs do I hold that enable me to do this work well? What of these values and beliefs are also inhibiting or blinding me from doing it well by others? Other supportive modalities such as coaching and mentoring can and do invite critical reflection on practice, and this can be effective in certain contexts or circumstances: for example, in the mentoring of early career teachers (Long et al., 2012) or in the coaching of new school leaders (Van Nieuwerburgh et al., 2020). As we have suggested, however, Professional Supervision is uniquely placed to engage with a broader range and diversity of affective ways of knowing and recognising of the dynamic flows of complex systems, people, and practices. As such, critical reflection is an important part, but not the whole, of the intention of Professional Supervision.

Imaginal Reflection

Millar's depiction of imaginal reflection attends to 'personal interaction, imagination, intuition, emotion and serendipity in practitioner experience' (Millar, 2018, p. 55). It evokes a reflexive turn beyond the rationality of critical reflection in that it 'includes noticing and appreciating evocative moments during the time of reflection itself – how one turns up in reflection'. It includes the 'personal impressions, images, thoughts, feelings, memories and fantasies and temptations that arise in the [actual] process of reflection' (Millar, 2018, p. 55). This kind of reflection demands more of the supervisee, in terms of recognising how and why they inhabit their practice. It draws attention to supervisees' capacities to work 'more as an intuitive experiencer than a detached observer and analyst' of their experience (Millar 2018, p. 56). Millar further explains that the 'purpose of attending to these experiences is to develop self-understanding, integrity and authenticity in our work which is important if practitioners [supervisees] are to nurture their sense of vocation' (Millar 2018, p. 57). He also cautions that imaginal reflection, if unchecked, 'can dissolve into personal truth/knowledge claims and even narcissistic self-absorption, raising the crucial question of what counts as rigour in imaginal reflection' (Millar 2018, p. 58).

Expanding beyond the essential questions of practice (what should I do?) and questions of effectiveness (what enables me to do it well?), imaginal reflection can draw school leaders to more existential reflections: what do I really want to do? These questions can risk becoming indulgent (navel-gazing), even counterproductive, if exercised without necessary rigour. Which brings us to Millar's fourth type of reflection for supervision purposes: ontological reflection which traditionally refers to philosophical or theological inquiry into the nature of being.

Ontological Reflection

Ontological reflection gets to the heart of vocation and helps to signify worldviews and ways of being not just in professional contexts, but in life.

> Ontological reflection pays careful attention to the particularities and nuances of a practitioner's ways of being in practice (their words, actions and reactions) and to what these reveal about who they are and how they perceive the world, as well as about the nature of their context and the work of their

profession. Ontological reflection's purpose is to support practitioners to grow in their practical wisdom or *phronesis*. (Millar, 2018, p. 65)

This kind of reflection can be the most demanding as it asks questions of true purpose and vocation. It leads the supervisee to consider: what is worth doing? In the case of school leaders, this kind of question is rarely asked of them. It can be vulnerable territory as it invites reflection on the connections and conversations between 'soul', role, and context in their lives (Paterson, 2019).

Each of the four modes of reflection identified by Millar is valid in Professional Supervision, depending on the context. Problems emerge, however, when compliance or competence cultures restrict the purpose of reflection solely to instrumental problem-fixing, performance management, or critique of critical events. Similarly, reflection 'concerned primarily with how we can access, reconcile and emancipate our ways of knowing' (Millar 2018, p. 65) can miss key opportunities to widen our lenses of understanding. It can dismiss, or worse avoid, the phases of discomfit that genuine deep learning sometimes require. Professional Supervision can, and must, be reflexive, drawing on the oft-neglected reflective intelligences which ironically are often latent in education spaces. Ontological reflection, as part of being reflexive, engages with 'our being in the world and with what we can and need to become if we are to be faithful to the people with whom we work, to the profession to which we belong and to ourselves as practitioners' (Millar, 2018, p. 65).

How Professional Supervision Has Developed

To support the case for Professional Supervision in education, it is important to recognise its genealogy with respect to its purpose, key conceptual frameworks, and signature practices. The widespread consensus is that it was first established in the 'helping' professions: that is, professions in human services and support, whether that be clinical in terms of physical and mental health care settings or pastoral in terms of spiritual care (Hawkins & McMahon, 2020). As a theory-informed practice, Professional Supervision is now widely accepted as a key registration and/or professional learning requirement in many clinical, health, and pastoral leadership professions. Moore describes the ways in which it was initially developed within the psychoanalysis field before being quickly adapted in various counselling and therapeutic sectors to support professionals in those fields. A third movement in the development of Professional Supervision more broadly, Moore writes, 'involved the incorporation of developmental models of how supervisor and supervisee learn, including the various social roles assumed in the supervisory relationship' (Moore, 2010, p. 167).

For the last decade, particularly in Australia, other disciplines – such as theology – have integrated Professional Supervision in support of the professional practice of leaders (Broughton, 2021). Contemporary understandings and practices of Professional Supervision have therefore been informed by, and at times emerged distinctively across, three broad disciplines: clinical, social work, and pastoral. Each contribution is distinct and contributes to the present integrated and transdisciplinary practice of Professional Supervision. We identify these contributions before returning to our own imaginal schema for Professional Supervision in education in Section 4.

Presence and Partnering: A Clinical Focus on Professional Relationships Being Protective

People meeting in the spirit of presence and partnership, is at the heart of supervision's intent in clinical settings. Detailed accounts of the contribution of clinical and counselling disciplines to the relational and ethical practices of Professional Supervision are provided by others, such as Liz Beddoe (2016) and Heather Fowlie (2016). In particular, Fowlie captures the essence of the clinical disciplines' contributions to supervision with her aptly titled chapter, 'Relational Supervision – A Two-Person Approach' (Fowlie, 2016).

The clinical emphasis on relationships that are safe, ethical, and protective (i.e. not abusive, manipulative, harmful, or coercive) is foundational to contemporary Professional Supervision. The importance of psychological safety at work has now become explicit in Australia's Workplace Health and Safety Act (Safe Work Australia, 2023), and is particularly important in those sectors in which professionals are dealing with institutional cultures of historical abuse or toxicity. No professional can flourish in an unsafe work environment, and too many workplaces (such as churches and faith-based organisations) remain unsafe and have failed as yet to reckon with toxic and abusive cultures and histories. The common phrase, 'you cannot be what you cannot see', is apt for many practitioners in pastoral contexts, for example, and is partly the reason behind the recommendation in parliamentary enquiries into institutional responses to sexual abuse (Commonwealth of Australia, 2017) that Professional Supervision be mandated for people in religious leadership roles. The clinical emphasis and contributions of Professional Supervision, both as a space for attending to the topic of safe and ethical practices, and as a process of modelling what safe and ethical practices look like in a relational encounter, has been critical to Professional Supervision's effectiveness and development across many disciplines. A safe environment is first seen and experienced in the supervision space. Carroll has been an important voice in bringing attention to the clinical field's contributions of presence and partnership into the supervision room of pastoral professions. He lists the supervisor's responsibilities to create a safe environment as:

1. Build in structure.
2. Contract clearly.
3. Provide rapport, warmth and openness.
4. Go slowly and tentatively (too much challenge too soon can destroy).
5. Begin to take small risks to show that it is safe.
6. Model appropriate self-disclosure and risk-taking.
7. Provide a lot of support.
8. Normalise what is happening.

(Carroll, 2014, p. 30)

Normalising reflexivity here is key. Supervisors are responsible for building trust and psychological safety so that deep learning – which can entail phases of vulnerability, honesty and discomfit – can occur. In the context of supervisor training, this is critical. Supervisor and psychotherapist Jack Finnegan, for example, interrogates the metaphor of space in clinical supervision, by employing Mikhail Bakhtin's dialogic theory to ensure supervisors become aware in their pedagogy and practice: 'What voice am I hearing? Whose voice am I hearing? What is really happening in this narration . . . How is it reconstructing my supervisee in the telling? How will it reconstruct me as I enter it in dialogue?' (Finnegan, 2010, p. 135). In these questions, the vital contributions of clinical practice to Professional Supervision practice are evident. Questioning becomes central to cultivating presence and embracing partnership in the effort to broaden supervisees' frames of reference. Other contributions from clinical fields include the important understandings and considerations of transference and other relational dynamics of learning-centred supervisory alliance.

Agency and Advocacy: A Social Work Focus on Agency within Professional Systems

If the contribution of clinical professions' knowledge underscores the need for psychological safety as both a practice and a purpose of supervision, this has not always meant an extension to questions of power with and within systems and cultures. Social work perspectives have sharpened this lens in Professional Supervision's development, with a focus on the potential of supervision to cultivate agency and advocacy in organisational life. For Karvinen-Niinikoski, Beddoe, Ruch, and Tsui (2017), the enduring value of Professional Supervision in social work contexts is the clear emphasis on critical reflection and 'helping to recognise and manage the fine balance between support and surveillance or managerial organisational dimensions' (Karvinen-Niinikoski et al., 2017, p. 53). Policy advocate Len Baglow refers to this function as both advocacy and mediation 'between the worker and the various systems that the worker needs to engage with' (Baglow, 2009, p. 355). In the Seven-Eyed Model supervision we practise, this awareness becomes explicit in Mode Seven of the supervisory conversation. The supervisor-as-ally facilitates not just awareness of the system and context, but awareness of the intention to maintain and develop professional agency in them. As such, the legacy and learnings of quality Professional Supervision from its practice in social work means 'supervision has been an important medium for strengthening professional identity, identifying coping strategies for personal survival and growth ... [and] securing both the quality of professional work and the wellbeing of practitioners' (Karvinen-Niinikoski et al., 2017, p. 64).

Vision and Vocation: A Pastoral World Focus on Professional Callings

The significant contribution of various practices of Professional Supervision within pastoral care and theology contexts has been a focus on purposeful calling. Supporting clarity of vision (looking again) and vocations of conviction (living again) is where supervisors in the pastoral sectors excel (Broughton, 2024). In my (Geoff's) initial contracting conversation with supervisees, I caution that I am liable to make every conversation a conversation about vocation. I am not surprised when the response is 'bring it on', even when I work outside the pastoral sector, for example with school principals. In professional contexts of such complexity and pressure, supervisees must (re)discover their *why*: their sense of vocational calling or purpose or, as I relate it to them, they simply won't last the distance. While key contemporary writers in education, like Biesta, may discuss the 'beautiful risk' of education (Biesta, 2013) from a philosophical perspective, the beautiful risk of educational leadership is similarly a compelling vocational call that Professional Supervision helps to both honour and unpack. From a similarly pastoral angle in the Quaker tradition, Parker J. Palmer writes of the need to align 'soul' and role in education vocation (Palmer, 2004). Professional Supervision takes Biesta's and Palmer's calls one step further to consider the exploration of soul and role *in context*.

Where Is Professional Supervision Now?

Back with the school leadership team, and my (Geoff's) own reflexive turn is instructive – for me as the supervisory facilitator, and for the group of supervisees as co-agents of their own professional learning. Critical reflection, it could be said, is natural and normal for educators. They enquire to understand. And we now know that good learning environments must provide psychological safety for that to happen in the first place. However, my initial instinct, along with many educators impacted by the complexities of their roles and the time pressures of their day, is to fast-track towards deciphering assumptions. Indeed, the principal admits her impatience with the opening reflections. Yet, my own awareness that a good, concise and academically rigorous definition wasn't what the group needed, occurred after the introductory pause and silence for breathing, body awareness, and sharing their twin horizons of intention.

My understanding of my own supervisor Bobby Moore's process framework assists in interpreting what is happening for the group: in choosing 'how I want to be' (or, 'what I commit my time and effort to') involves 'wearing your theory lightly' in order to discern which intuitions are actually resourcing my practice.

We shift phase in the session, and the role of the group is to be conversational about what they wish to focus on in this time together. They bring their own critical capacities for making meaning and making decisions about their focus – what Moore describes as think feelingly or feel thinkingly. This resonance between emotional and theoretical intelligences is critical because we easily choose one to the exclusion of the other.

The seduction for educators is that we can instinctively move into teaching mode (providing good definitions) without first reflecting on how we want to be. The initial personal reflection, therefore, invited the participants to be curious about their curiosity. Were they committed to the kind of listening that ignites the mind and expands each other's professional perspective in their work together? Or were they present only to instrumental reflection – intent on critiquing past successes and failures as data to plan the future.

An important phase of Moore's process framework anchors on learning that is transformational, not merely informational. Perhaps this provokes apprehension and anxiety among educators? The focus on future action is as essential as it is elusive – Moore asks 'what I am going to do differently as a result of my new, critical awareness?' Educators feel this tension at the end of every class or lecture, the end of every school year or semester, and particularly when students are graduating: what are my students going to do with their new, critical awareness? At this moment, the reflexive turn is critical.

Moore proposes three elements in practically fostering reflexivity in supervision: noticing assumptions (intuitions), bringing them to mind (intention), and making them available for critical reflection (investigation). The task of fostering curiosity then becomes central: which intentions are resourcing my practice/work?; choosing how I want to be (i.e. what I commit my time and effort to); and translate thought into action. Practical reflexivity therefore enables transformational learning and action: what I am going to do differently as a result of my new, critical awareness? (Moore, 2017).

How a supervisor facilitates this reflexivity is dependent on the quality of their listening. Are they listening primarily to interrupt – the default of quick-thinking leaders with a problem-solving mindset? Are they listening to understand – and thereby prioritising their own curiosity and learning above that of the supervisee they are they to serve? Or are they genuinely there to listen to ignite – to facilitate the supervisee's own thinking about their thinking; their own assumptions, intuitions, intentions, and actions?

Together, we (Geoff and the school executive team) move through levels of robust, respectful, and resonant conversation.

Initially our conversation is robust in its controlled discussion whereby people are listening to interrupt. Teachers are familiar with these types of discussions in the classroom (and staffroom) and clearly enjoy the energy and creativity of these energised and increasingly fast flows of thought, critique, and ideas. But as the work of Kline and Moore reminds us, the value of this can diminish over time. How is this replicating usual patterns of thinking fast, on the run? How is it potentially diminishing the deeper insight that processes of Professional Supervision affords?

Our second level of conversation is respectful. It is skilful conversation whereby people are listening to understand. Most school leaders already practise this respectful listening with colleagues, students, parents, and other key stakeholders, but again both Kline and Moore acknowledge the limiting nature of listening to understand for becoming reflexive. As crucial as empathy and emotional resonance are for school leaders professionally, it is not the goal of Professional Supervision to merely empathise and understand each other. Of course, conversations that go beyond doing reflection *to* being reflexive *should never fall below the skilful 'respectful listening' needed to understand, but they must aspire towards next level 'listening to ignite': listening that enables attention to the 'what else?', 'what's missing?', 'what's my assumption/role/intention in that?', 'what's the worth in that?'. This quality of conversation, arising from 'listening to ignite', is one of deep resonance. It brings forth generative interaction, where people are listening to ignite each other's minds.*

Continuing Legacies

What we know now as Professional Supervision has been around for over 40 years, and its current frameworks have evolved and been influenced by the diverse professional contexts in which it has been practised. As a learning endeavour, Professional Supervision simultaneously evolves through entanglements of inner discernment ('soul') with relational acts ('role' and 'context'). Reflexivity arises in conversational and creative encounters of noticing, considering, and consolidating.

At its quality best, Professional Supervision engages ontological ways of knowing that invite supervisees to be reflexive rather than merely do reflection solely for instrumentalist means and ends. This capacity is reliant on the qualities of *presence and partnering* derived from relational practices of clinical supervision, *agency and advocacy* from contextual social work approaches, and attention to *vocation and calling* as experienced in pastoral settings of supervision. How might Professional Supervision in the field of education both inform and be informed by ongoing developments such as these?

In the next section, we draw on the richness of Professional Supervision's cross disciplinary practice to date, contemporary paradigms of assemblage-thinking and emergence in education, and our own experience of supervising and teaching educational leaders, to offer a schema for Professional Supervision in education. As much as possible, we anchor this thinking in the practical and preamble it with the following testimony of sorts; one that gets to the simplicity beyond the complexity of Professional Supervision:

Beyond what I do
(the practice of leading a school),
how I think about what I do
(critical reflection on practice to lead a school well),
lies a way of being in my profession
(how I show up as a school leader in everything I do).

4 CURA for Education Leaders: A Schema for Professional Supervision in Education

So far, we have:

- considered the role and challenges of reflective practice in education
- made a case for educational leaders to *be reflexive* rather than just *do reflection*
- provided an overview of the key practice concepts and frameworks for reflexive Professional Supervision in and across disciplines

In this section, we:

- propose a schema of Professional Supervision in education anchored in four key conditions for quality practice:
    - Curiosity
    - Unlearning
    - Attunement
    - Resonance

- establish a systems-thinking approach that regards schools as dynamic assemblages, and focus our attention on the work of education leaders

In this text, our experiences of leading, learning, and supervising in complex, multidimensional contexts have informed our writing. Our interests in Professional Supervision derive from its effectiveness in such settings, particularly as a process-oriented, multi-lensed framework for being reflexive not just doing reflection. As we have argued in Section 2, Professional Supervision creates space for engaging with matters of purpose, vision, and ethical responsibility that take educational leaders beyond reflection that is solely instrumental or technical in intent. This opportunity to attend to the role and 'soul' in context via a trusted supervisory alliance appears to us to be enhancing and sustaining a sense of professional agency, vocation, and wellbeing with the principals we supervise and teach.

Professional Supervision has been shown to be beneficial in a range of human service and 'helping' professions that require complex navigation of people, projects, professional standards, and systems. As Section 3 has outlined, supervision's integration in three professional fields in particular has informed the evolution of its ongoing practice in others. The clinical sector has sharpened Professional Supervision's relational pedagogy as interpersonal interaction; the social work field's foundations in questions of agency and power have added new lenses for thinking and dialogue; and the pastoral community's attention to matters of vocation and calling has contributed to ongoing understandings of how to engage with ethics and bigger questions of purpose and value in supervisory encounters.

We have two entwined aims for this final section. Firstly, we seek to contribute to the continuing development of Professional Supervision by making explicit the integration of contemporary educational thinking on our practice. Secondly, we distil four key conditions for quality Professional Supervision in educational leadership specifically, and in the education sector more broadly. These are curiosity, unlearning, attunement, and resonance. You will note we call these conditions, rather than principles, although in some cases they are both and could be used interchangeably. We choose to refer to them as conditions to highlight their value – for we could not practise quality supervision with educational leaders without them. Why? For us, as practitioners, it is important to recognise that Professional Supervision with school leaders means engaging with supervisees who are leading context-specific learning within an educational organisation: they are themselves learning professionals. Expectations and assumptions about what constitute good learning are therefore a little more entrenched (including sometimes being narrower) than in other professional contexts. This alerts us to a responsibility to ensure Professional Supervision is entered into with integrity and authenticity to its ontologically oriented intentions. For us, this means being explicit in our preparation and contracting with supervisees that we will be reflexive (not just reporting or recalling) together in our sessions and that this calls on conversation born of curiosity (not just compliance) and a willingness to unlearn (not just affirm). Furthermore, schools are sites of multiple and multi-directional flows of effect and affect. Personal, social, and emotional interactions are constantly in flow among the people, places, policies, and procedures of a school community. Leaders' everyday decisions, choices, and responsibilities, without exception, have an ethical imperative. The effectiveness of Professional Supervision with educational leaders is therefore conditional upon their attunement and resonance with these flows, so that reflexive processes can be ignited. We propose that only then can Professional Supervision enhance practice and counter the habits of business-as-usual and its quick-fix tendencies which, as our supervisees note and our own experience testifies, are not always in service of wise action or sustainable leadership.

Our writing takes a more speculative turn here as we offer insights about how the conditions of curiosity, unlearning, resonance, and attunement could be cultivated. In taking an imaginal and reflexive stance ourselves, we invite you to join us in contemplating questions of what is and what if, rather than what's (as yet) proven. We consider how these conditions show up in supervision's places, presence, practices, and purpose in school contexts. To offer this as a schema fulfils our intention to draw on our own capacities for reflective intelligence to organise and communicate the ideas that excite and stretch us at this point in time. It also invites us to be open and somewhat vulnerable in serving a new field of endeavour, and we do so in the hope it may inspire further research and development of supervision in the education sector.

Before launching into our prospective play with this schema – *CURA for Educational Leaders* – we provide an important preamble to define our context: the school. We do not refer to schools as sites, a set of buildings, or even as communities for the purpose of this exploration, but as assemblages. We then draw on writings from a range of disciplines and sources that have informed and inspired us to consider the conditions of curiosity, unlearning, resonance, and attunement as the basis for Professional Supervision in educational leadership.

Schools as Assemblages

As many before us have argued, we are living a 'VUCA' world: one of volatility, uncertainty, complexity, and ambiguity (Bennett & Lemoine, 2014; Bawany, 2016; Taguma & Gabriel, 2018; Panthalookaran 2022). While each era in recorded human history could make similar claims, and while it is undeniable that marginalised communities and those in resource-impoverished and violent contexts live with VUCA daily, the planetary trajectory of climate emergency and the associated threat of political, social, and financial systems collapse make this current situation at scale for humanity particularly challenging. Previously pervasive modernist narratives born of the industrial complex that celebrate individuals' quest to ever-improve, ever-progress, and ever-accumulate are becoming increasingly hollow and violently troubling. While more critically hopeful pluriversal and regenerative thought and action are spreading (Brown, 2017; Wheatley & Frieze, 2018; Escobar, 2020; Macy, 2021), the current situation raises questions about the purpose and value of schooling. How do we define, chart, and measure learning when the future is unknown? What should the experience of school or being schooled be for? These questions may seem alarmist to those with the fortune to live in communities where the importance of a good education is a given and schools are resourced adequately to do so. But the broader remit of these questions are ontological, with practical implications for the work and wellbeing of school principals now and into the future. For as the uncertain impacts of a VUCA world – and a responsive 'reworlding' of the ways we know and learn together – begin to manifest locally, schools are sites where the tensions about future-readiness are magnifying. Schools are prime intergenerational sites of meaning-making and for holding the educational paradox of addressing the human urge for certainty while developing the knowledge and skills to live without it.

This situation calls for an important rethink about how leaders lead for and with agency in complex and uncertain times – and how they are supported to do so. As Strom, Haas, Danzig, Martinez, and McConnell have argued, with respect to the role of school leadership in 'post-truth' times, it requires a shift to 'viewing the world/their work as interactive assemblages, rather than as something done by individual actors with absolute agency' (Strom et al., 2018, p. 271). School leaders have already experienced aspects of this altered view of agency with the COVID-19 pandemic, whereby they 'navigated multiple tensions simultaneously, between autonomy and accountability, well-being, and workload' (Torrance et al., 2023, p. 1108 citing Netolicky, 2020). In finding ways to lead that were not business-as-usual, principals relied on co-action and co-agency with others to manage the uncertainty and affective load (Anderson & Weiner, 2023; Da-as, Oadach, &

Schechter, 2023; Thomson & Greany, 2024). Onward from the peak of that crisis, much has been learnt about the need to cultivate school leaders' expanded sense of co-agency in navigating social, political, organisational, and personal aspects (Chen-Levi et al., 2024) of leadership, but we've yet to learn *how*. School principals still report that they find themselves professionally lonely and ill-supported by the systems they serve (Gorrell & De Nobile, 2023), despite the significant learnings from the pandemic. Systemic priorities for supporting leadership life cycles appear to be more front-ended with concentrated attention on principals' initial management of the procedural and technocratic parts of their work (likened to proficiencies in knowing *what* decisions need to be made, *when*, and to *what ends*). Yet, for mid and late career leaders, it appears hands-on support is less available for grappling with the complexities, and potentially more vocationally intensive questions, of *how* decisions are made, *for whom*, and *why*.

In working with established school leaders, we as supervisors are finding that Professional Supervision is offering opportunities for reflexivity on the entwined effective and affective flows of work: that is, a desired opportunity to move beyond reflection on the necessary instrumental aspects of their role towards engagement with the less tangible and extrinsically measurable (Kidson, 2024). Embracing this noticing, we adopt Strom et al.'s call to utilise assemblage-thinking as a generative frame of reference that acknowledges the ways in which professional and personal beliefs, standards, practices, and ethics entangle. We suggest this frame is necessary to honour the interactive flows of affect and effect, feeling and meaning, sensing and making sense, that influence and are influenced by the work of principals. Linear causality is impossible to identify or justify in the work of school leadership, despite political, bureaucratic and curricula remits in the education sector that presume otherwise. The quality of principals' understanding and navigation of the everyday inter- and intra-actions with these flows not only impacts their own sense of agency, value, and wellbeing, but the agency, value, and wellbeing of the teachers, students and communities they serve.

While the language of assemblages may not as yet be commonplace in the sector, for many principals what's at stake *without* this recognition of the multiple and multi-directional flows of school life, is the self-described 'soul' of their work: not defined in religious or esoteric terms, but as an identification with their vocational commitment, sustenance, and sense of purpose as they navigate these assemblages. Many come to realise that their choices and actions as leaders can activate, resist or impact the many and various dynamic flows of the school. Like an ecology, everything influences, in some way, everything else. Nothing is unidirectional and nothing is the sole work of an individual.

As noted in previous sections, Professional Supervision seeks to 'interrupt practice' (Ryan, 2004, p. 44) and, in doing so, we argue it acknowledges the more 'emergent, collectivist, systems-level' perspectives (Strom et al., 2018, p. 271) called for at this time. In the models of supervisory practice we've experienced and that we discuss here, Professional Supervision works explicitly with the idea that a supervisee's professional practice is composed of a 'variety of people, things, ideas, and power flows' (Strom et al., 2018, p. 271). Therefore, agency relies not on exercising power individually, but in cultivating leaders' capacities to 'analyze the ways that the multiple moving parts of the educational organization they lead work together to produce particular conditions' (Strom et al., 2018, p. 271). It is in finding the smooth spaces (Deleuze & Guattari, 1988) – and the knowing that these multiple moving parts have generative influence and impact on each other – that enables more flexibility and opportunity to disrupt the status quo and potentially 'do things differently' (Strom et al., 2018, p. 271).

For us, the Seven-Eyed Model of Professional Supervision aligns with assemblage-thinking. Rather than perceiving professional practice as defined or constrained by the system, leaders are invited to examine their own and other's fluid positionalities and perspectives. In the process of facilitated conversation, they are encouraged to realise their capacity to be professionally agentic – and thereby co-agentic – in guiding certain flows of effect and affect with and for others. Cultivating and activating agency this way, through being reflexive, is how we come to notice and value Professional Supervision as a pedagogy for and of change.

With assemblage-thinking underpinning our own ways of knowing practically and theoretically in this text, we now turn to our prospective schema for Professional Supervision in the education sector. While our focus here is on school principals, we see saliences for all levels and roles of teaching and leadership in education systems. Drawing on our current experience working intensively with principals, both in supervision and in teaching about supervision, we attend to four conditions we see as necessary for quality Professional Supervision. These are not necessarily *pre*-conditions – we acknowledge that they are always already in play, so to speak, in supervisory practice. Rather, our aim is to discuss them as crucial to supervision practice in education. Our conceptual experiment here is to attend to each condition in relation to the place, presence, practice, and purpose of Professional Supervision and see how they land.

We begin – reflexively of course – with why CURA? What is the intention?

CURA for Leaders of Education

'CURA'
Latin – to help, care (also: cura te ipsum 'take care of yourself' and cura et valeas 'take care of your health'. Here in Australia, mihi cura futture 'mine is the care of the future')
Spanish – healing (also for priest/pastor)
Slang – to have fun
Urban dictionary – a 'fix' (usually heroin)

Our teaching and supervisory sessions with educators over the last two years have been deeply affecting. More so than in any other sectors we have worked, the relief expressed by principals about having found a process that seems to address their individual needs and collective concerns at this time has been often visceral.

If there is one thing that a deep learning and practice in supervision has taught us, it is that there are many and diverse ways of knowing. Here, our experiential way of knowing counts and this is captured in our wordplay with the acronym CURA. For us, **c**uriosity, **u**nlearning, **r**esonance, and **a**ttunement are the conditions for quality supervision in the education sector. But, more than that, the spirit of supervision is captured in the etymology of the word CURA. We've read and heard principals' deep commitment to care (*Latin origin of CURA*): they care for others as leaders, they recognise the need to care for themselves, and ultimately we recognise our collectivised view of the teaching profession in the saying, 'mihi cura futture' ('mine is the care of the future'). The intention to care is what brings so many to the profession of teaching in the first place and here we see this projected onto Professional Supervision, particularly for educational leaders as a way to care for peers and others.

In supervision, we've been witness-bearers to stories where people have found the act of talking a kind of healing (*Spanish use of CURA*) of difficult experience. Through facilitated processes of supervision that widen the lens of understanding, the aha moments for supervisees can sometimes be profound, and also fun (*CURA is slang for fun*). Sharing in the laughter and relief of seeing something differently, or seeing oneself anew, is not uncommon in Professional Supervision. Neither are tears – of recognition, unlearning, or release. And, yes, this can feel loosely like a fix (*urban use of word*) – an affective turn or frame that is rarely given space and time in the professional movement of the day.

We take care not to proselytise in our playfulness here. The empirical evidence will in time accumulate and accommodate the needs of those wanting proof that Professional Supervision 'works' before they try. But we write in a phase of emergence and creativity of this practice in school settings. This affords us certain freedoms to be authentic to supervision's reflexive intent.

Condition #1: Curiosity

Many educators will be aware of the role curiosity plays in educational engagement and motivation. What may be less known is that curiosity has multiple dimensions and, therefore, can have multiple flows of thought and action. Ultimately, curiosity can be leveraged in generative ways for engaged learning. Building on our foundational understanding of Professional Supervision as a learning endeavour, the first condition we propose here is curiosity for both supervisor and supervisee. As Carroll affirms, 'Curiosity is our starting point in supervision. As curious beings, we wonder and ask why. . . . We ask questions of ourselves and of our practice in order to learn' (Carroll, 2014, p. 140). The key challenge for school leaders enculturated in 'thinking fast' is, 'Can we move from instant evaluation to contemplative curiosity?' (Carroll, 2014, p. 140).

With hyper-accountability and measurement imperatives impacting the culture of contemporary schools, it is unsurprising that the art of curiosity is more often mired, rather than partnered, by the science of evaluation. In an instrumentalist paradigm of learning, what is measurable is what by default gets valued. Teachers, leaders, researchers, and learners know this, for better or worse, and can become preoccupied with evidence and evaluation: 'What worked before – it will work again'. 'How well did that work?' 'What do we need to do to improve?' 'What's next?' For some aspects of school life, evaluative data-lead reflection and analysis are necessary. What we are hearing established school principals say, though, is that the demands of performative and improvement agendas are leaving little time and energy for the curiosity-fuelled questions that are more pertinent to them and their role. They express the yearning to consider 'Why?' 'What else?' 'What if?'

Hence, seasoned principals can find themselves in default habits of premature cognitive commitment (Langer, 1989) when it comes to beginning Professional Supervision, due to working so long within systems that privilege counting over curiosity. A tendency to expedite solutions-thinking serves the *effective* flow of work but does little for the *affective* dimensions of what it means to lead and learn. Value in the alignments of 'soul', role, and context in leadership diminishes.

Yet humans' impetus to learn – a survival strategy we learn as infants – derives from processes of information-seeking and experience-seeking. In studies of curiosity, these processes are known as epistemic curiosity (a cognitive drive and exploration to know, evoked by realising there's an unknown); and perceptual curiosity (a seeking or encounter with new sensory stimuli leading to an exploratory drive to experience and to feel) (Berlyne, 1954, 1960; McNary, 2023). While there is scholarly debate on whether curiosity is a state or trait, we consider it here as a condition for supervisory practice. Whether it is a psychological or philosophical underpinning to understandings of curiosity that is taken, it is universally accepted that humans are motivated not only by a want to cognitively know an unknown, but to also experience new stimuli for learning. Curiosity isn't only fuelled by the want of an answer to a question, but humans require and seek new, diverse, intense, and complex sensations, experiences, and ways of thinking to grow (Reio et al., 2006). It can be lively and can enlarge a field of vision, while at the same time avoid or redirect reductive thinking (Zuss, 2011). Furthermore, a critical curiosity, like critical reflection, becomes 'a name for the experience of futurity ... an opening without determination, a becoming different, resisting representation and fixed subjectivity' (Zuss, 2011, p. 84). As such, curiosity can be a 'restless force' (2011, p. x), requiring 'pedagogical encounter with an unfinished, open-ended totality of the possible' (2011, p. x). How, then, to harness and direct this restless force for good, and not be overwhelmed with potential open-endedness? How to find and sustain curiosity and clarity in equal partnership?

Professional Supervision both invites and ignites curiosity. An understanding of the different types of curiosity can enable Professional Supervision to meet school leaders at their own learning edges. The practices of supervision can offer opportunities for an urge to need to know and *make sense* of something, at the same time as acknowledging and bringing focus to the affect-oriented *sensing* of things. Supervisees can be encouraged to tap into their perceptual and sensory curiosity – 'what this looked and felt like', 'what did I make of this?' – rather than rush with the assessment impulse – 'what was good and bad?', 'what will make it better?' This alerts us to the distinction, once again, between doing reflection as an exercise of assessing and being reflexive as process of learning. Professional Supervision urges supervisees to become curious about their knowledge and experience, and onwards to curiously explore the frames of reference they cage these in. To invite contemplation and questioning of not just 'the truth', but the potential for 'many truths' is conditional upon curiosity.

It's our fourth session, I (Mary Ann) ask Lee what she'd like to bring to supervision today. She's having a difficult time with two of her executive team who 'just don't get on'. 'It's frustrating, I'm so exhausted by their pettiness and conflict'. Attuning to Lee's affective flows of frustration and exhaustion, I acknowledge this as a challenge. She replies she just wants to fix the problem but then she hesitates, takes a breath. After numerous sessions together, she's remembering that we're not here to find quick-fixes or share tried and true strategies, but we're here to be curious, to 'think on our thinking'. 'Weeell, I can't make them besties, but I need to make them work better together'. 'That sounds like a really strong need.' I pause for a moment. 'Lee, that frustration and exhaustion – what toll is that taking?' Lee jumps in: 'A massive toll – I'm becoming short with them and taking on the jobs myself that they can't manage to do together'. 'So, I'm curious – what's the toll on them?' 'Well, none really. I'm picking up the pieces all the time'. There is a bit of an aha moment – for both of us. 'Where might the frustration be really sitting?' As our session continues, we get more curious together about where the seeds of frustration lie and Lee shares that she's getting frustrated with herself in not finding a solution to their interpersonal tension which is, ultimately, beyond her control. Lee comes to the insight herself, that maybe her way of dealing with it by redirecting their work tasks to herself to get things done is not wise action. 'What's the real need here?' There's a long silence. Quietly, Lee says 'To feel respected'. We take a moment to check in and re-contract with each other. 'How is that landing for you? Is it something you'd like to continue exploring in the context of your professional role here with me? Or are you sensing it's a bigger piece of more personal work that might be best engaged with with a close friend or the skills of a counsellor?' Lee elects to use the new noticing as a lens on her experience of chairing meetings with her team over the next while. It's not a solution, but it's a learning. Clarity has emerged for Lee on a vital part of her professional practice which may have been missed in a race to make things better, without first being curious about why.

Exploring Lee's dilemma with her under the condition of curiosity, invited her to formulate her own question-seeking questions. Here, curiosity was not a state or trait to be attained or developed, but an underpinning to help access, articulate, and generate new meaning *of* experience and *in* experience for Lee. As such, it became something akin to an enquiry-based pedagogy of and for change in her professional practice. Zuss suggests that in education, 'theoretical and conceptual growth can only occur in the flows, turns, and circuits of thought and becoming' (p. 140). Curiosity is therefore 'kindling' for 'intensities of thinking' to occur (Zuss, 2011, p. 140).

As Carroll attests in relation to Professional Supervision, the ability to be curious in times of uncertainty 'is in itself a creative process' (2014, p. 89). By offering a trusted and confidential relationship, and invitation to contemplative curiosity across experience and time, Professional Supervision can serve to interrupt practice and ignite creativity, not just assessment, in the face of professional challenge. The case of Lee shows us it is important not to mistake a quick solution for clarity. For while solution-finding can be the initial impetus for seeking professional support like supervision, clarity arrived for Lee under the condition of curiosity: the lesson here being that short-cutting to solutions may also short-circuit the reflexivity that honours the rich, complex and multi-dimensional qualities of professional practice and leadership. What makes professional supervision so enabling as a contemporary approach to supporting school leaders, is this opportunity to interrupt business-as-usual's assessment of good or bad:

We can evaluate later. For now we stop and wonder. And we do that with kindness and compassion. Not a kindness and compassion that denies what has happened, or becomes overly optimistic, but one that allows for humanity, frailty, understanding and acceptance (Carroll, 2014, p. 140).

Condition #2: Unlearning

As we've seen, curiosity is not just a cognitive act. It engages the parts of us that 'sense' things, as much as the part that wants to 'make sense' of things. If quality Professional Supervision is therefore conditional upon curiosity, then affective dimensions of being disoriented ('I've never looked at it this way before') or discomforted ('Gosh, I don't know what I was thinking') need also to be welcomed. These affects of the learning labour of supervision are just as important as the choice of wise action that may follow. This is where our second condition of unlearning comes into play. This is not to suggest Professional Supervision is about making problems, but it is recognition that getting to the edges of our own knowledge and understanding can come with some challenge and some disorientation. Our condition #2 is therefore that all learning invites unlearning.

Professional Supervision is often described as a process of widening the lens of understanding. In doing so, supervisees can experience some disquiet in themselves when entrenched cultures, habits, or business-as-usual practices come under the condition of curiosity. Arrival at new insights can mean that established expertise, knowledge, or familiar frames of reference are tested. As Carroll reminds us, 'Learning from experience can cause disequilibrium' (2014, p. 126).

At its simplest, unlearning can be described as the process of letting go of assumptions, beliefs, or learned practices that no longer serve or open the way for new paradigms of knowledge or new lenses on experience to emerge (Macdonald, 2002; McWilliam, 2008; Tlostanova & Mignolo, 2012; Grisold & Kaiser, 2017). In Professional Supervision, unlearning can work as both a condition for, and result of, genuinely and vulnerably engaging in processes of being reflexive. It can have affective implications for a supervisee's view of themselves as a learner, and as a professional. It can challenge, expand, and invite deep noticings of self and personal identity: for to see a long-held belief or way of knowing for its limitations and biases can be confronting and disorienting.

Some years ago, I (Mary Ann) led an interdisciplinary team of colleagues teaching in the fields of education, social work, philosophy, sociology, and the arts in a project to explore what it means to be a mentor. Our initial goal was to create a mentoring programme that might be supportive and creatively interesting for early career social workers and teachers. We began with a commitment to being reflexive ourselves – that is, being curious together about what mentoring had looked like in the past for us and what we could each bring to this practical endeavour. Our own reflective practice as a team led us to unexpected places, however. We found ourselves engaged with questions of expertise and knowledge: how they were culturally inflected and valued differently in different contexts, and how they emerged individually for us in response to experiences of culture, self-efficacy, belonging, and professional challenge. We soon came to realise we had become more interested in the reflexive challenges of unravelling what was assumed to be so good about 'expertise and experience' in workplaces and how it was valued. We came to many shared moments of discomfit and disorientation as we reconsidered our project's goals and found ourselves far more engaged in processes of unlearning what is good teaching and effective mentoring, and how it relates to professional growth. Much of this sat outside the regulatory and performative focus of the systems and sectors we and our imagined mentoring programme were working in. In our troubled but generative 'thinking about thinking', we came to realise that

> while there are aspects of our knowledge, beliefs and practices that we can reimagine and reenvision in unlearning, we need to also recognise that our own disruptions will surface in relation to external impositions that might be concrete and unbending. The scope for change co-existing with the parameters of context, is an important insight for managing fluid but sustainable professional identities (McLeod et al., 2020, p. 193).

On considering the many modes of mentoring as learning, we forewent our original aim of creating a programme, instead to explore how unlearning might be supported as a means of sustaining ongoing professional practice whereby there are external rigidities but also contexts of constant flux (Gupta, Boland, & Aron, 2017). As the inspiration of the teachings of thirteenth-century Zen Buddhist writer Dōgen offered us, unlearning can be the practice of awakening, and in many ways, we came to value that the two (unlearning and awakening) are the same (Dōgen, 2007).

Fast forward some years, and I (Mary Ann) find myself engaged in Professional Supervision, as a practice that proactively and explicitly invites unlearning for supervisors as well as supervisees. For me, it's a condition – or perhaps more so a gateway – to resonance and attunement. A threshold to engaging with the discomfits of the heart and 'soul' of what we do in sustaining vocational integrity and commitment.

Condition #3: Resonance

I (Geoff) know when things resonate. A good supervisor knows when something resonates for their supervisee and, in response, will slow the pace of the conversation, pause, and invite consideration of the resonance more deeply. Here we argue it can be both a condition for, and outcome of, quality Professional Supervision. But what do we mean when we use the language of resonance in supervision and everyday language, such as 'that resonates'?

The concept of resonance, emerging from music and the arts, suggests connections, reverberations, and a creative response. In English, resonate finds its etymological root in Latin, *resonare,* meaning sound again. Sociologist Hartmut Rosa proposes the antidote to contemporary life's experience of alienation and acceleration is not merely slowing down but finding resonance. Resonant relationships, he argues, 'presuppose a kind of mutual, rhythmic oscillation' (Rosa, 2019, p. 26). This relationship can happen between a supervisor and supervisee, but more interestingly here, it can be resonance with an idea or another person or a way of seeing and sensing. Resonance can only happen with deep noticing and, while slowing down may offer better opportunities for deep noticing, it is not reliant on it.

This is useful for busy and pressured school leaders to know. For while supervision is an invitation to slow down, pause, notice, and reflect – and therefore be attractive as a life-giving oasis in the middle of back-to-back appointments – time pressure and multi-tasking are unavoidable in school leadership. Real and sustained slowing down is not compatible with the life and calling of a principal. So, what does resonance offer? How does it help?

In Rosa's more recent work, provocatively engaging with the 'uncontrollability' of the world, he deepens an understanding of resonance by highlighting the difference between self-efficacy and control. In large systems that prioritise compliance and control, Rose offers an alternative whereby 'the basic mode of vibrant human existence consists not in exerting control over things but in resonating with them, making them respond to us – thus experiencing self-efficacy – and responding to them in turn' (Rosa, 2020, p. 31).

In professional supervision conversations with senior leaders across a range of professions, the very idea of the difference between control and self-efficacy (dare I say it?), *resonates.*

For Rosa, resonance transcends itself as a metaphor to become a mode of relationship, with four exemplary characteristics: being affected; self-efficacy; adaptive transformation; and uncontrollability (Rosa, 2020, p. 32–49). These characteristics suggest the four practices that Professional Supervision offers school leaders: listening to ignite, leaning into agency, learning reflexively, and leading in and through complexity. These practices will be further developed next.

In the world of the arts, where resonance also finds a home, prominent theatre director Anne Bogart observes that 'clutter in the theatre space ... *prevent[s]* resonance' (Bogart, 2021, p. 4). Bogart argues that resonance is essential to the creative encounter because it is the 'thread that evokes a response and, in general, is understood as a quality that makes something personally meaningful and valuable' (Bogart, 2021, p. 5). Wryly, Bogart also notes 'that the decrease of resonance ... is called *dullness*' (Bogart, 2021, p. 6). Experienced school leaders may again resonate with the dullness of a busy routine and take heart from Bogart's creative proposals for igniting resonance: for example, in creative experiments with transforming and combining; adding, reshaping, and remixing (Bogart, 2021, pp.77–78).

Resonance in supervision can and must be characterised by reciprocity and mutual transformation. Although the demands of school leadership can sound more like a cacophony of competing cries and crises, can we find deeper resonance with and between them? To find 'mutual, rhythmic oscillation' with the assemblage of flows, choices, and actions that comprises a principal's day, the fourth co-condition of attunement also matters.

Condition #4: Attunement

Attunement can be described fundamentally as a neurobiological process that starts in mirror neurons (Siegel, 2007). Mirror neurons are central to the development of empathy and affect our emotions: if I observe someone crying, I myself will probably experience sadness. This attunement, according to Siegel, can be sensed by another person, thereby also creating resonance. For Siegel, 'resonance ... is the functional outcome of attunement that allows us to feel felt by another person' (Siegel, 2007, p. 167). The importance of intention is striking, and again has strong implications for supervision. Intention, and the capacity to attune to intention, 'form "the underlying 'glue" that directs attention, motivates action, and processes the nature of our actions' (Siegel, 2007, p. 178).

As discussed in earlier sections, the act of doing reflection involves noticing and considering. To deepen and extend this to being reflexive requires attunement to self and to others. This, Siegel argues, 'creates coherence in the mind' (Siegel, 2007, p. 193). Whereas much literature on reflective practice in education following Dewey prioritises the reflective intelligence needed for doing reflection, Siegel's research suggests that greater coherence and clarity are found through attunement, thereby proving itself to be an indispensable condition for reflexivity. Furthermore, Siegel's findings show that 'such attuned relationships promote resilience and longevity' (Siegel, 2007, p. xiv).

As we indicated in Section 3, attunement is evidenced in 'body regulation, attuned communication, emotional balance, response flexibility, empathy, self-knowing awareness, and fear modulation' (Siegel, 2007, p. 191). These bear a resemblance to the philosophical and artistic framings of resonance and offer us deeper insights about the connections that exist beyond semantics. It could reasonably be argued on the back of this evidence that attunement and resonance between people in supervision help modify each person's internal state (including their affective experience) towards wellbeing.

To cultivate attunement requires a degree of curiosity, humility, and unknowing. It can mean unlearning assumptions and beliefs that may have solidified perceptions of oneself, others, or even what an ideal learning encounter might look like. How then is resonance and attunement to be practically understood and cultivated in Professional Supervision? Alongside curiosity and unlearning, how do they show up in the places, presence, practices, and purpose of Professional Supervision for school leaders?

The sheer complexity of school leadership can subvert or distract from the deeper work of supervision as CURA, particularly in group supervision. One of the school executives was grappling with a range of issues across the school which impacted on the executive to different degrees. A common thread began to emerge for the leaders as they reflected together: when to lean in (with capable, yet near-capacity staff) and when to step back. The principal was last in the group to reflect and brought to the group a range of threats to the school. Internally, a recent on-site crisis had turbo-charged the school's need for higher risk management. Externally, a funding crunch posed as an existential threat to the school's continuing viability. These were just two of the issues named by the principal as pressing in on her as school leader. Would the group lean in or step back?

The group's curiosity, *however, revealed the executive members (who were well aware of each threat) had under-appreciated the cumulative impact on the principal. While each and every issue needed further reflection (and eventually real-world solutions), the experienced school leaders had already begun* unlearning *the ingrained habit of problem solving for each other. A surprising and powerful* resonance *emerged for the principal in this reflective space. The leader realised she must remain courageous in the face of the multiple threats. The single, greatest (and most immediate) risk to the school – and where group was most empowered to act purposively – was the principal's courage. The group was* attuned *to the principal's vulnerability, and through empathy, encouragement and recommitment to solidarity with, and support of, the principal, the session ended with a surprisingly hopeful mood.*

The CURA of supervision for school leaders is not a cure all. CURA, as we have experienced many times, facilitates the supervision conversation between soul, role, and context. As illustrated earlier, many school leaders face complexities that challenge their commitment to the role. CURA provides a way to integrate both soul (e.g. courage) and context (e.g. internal and external threats) into the supervision conversation.

CURA Places for Supervision

Following Rosa's invitation to see resonance as the antidote to busyness and acceleration, we propose that supervision be primarily considered as a *place*, rather than a time. Here, we are influenced by First Nations' perspectives, rather than Western constructs of linear time (and linear progression towards ends): in other words, the *place* of energy, attention, movement, and abiding. Over the last decade I (Geoff) have been privileged to work alongside several *Arrernte* elders and traditional custodians in central Australia, bearing witness to the primacy of place in their law, culture, and spirituality. One of those elders, Margaret *Kemarre* Turner ('MK'), expresses this 'connection' alternatively as a 'root' and a 'tie' and 'it holds all of us' (Turner, 2010, p. 115). Recently, Mary Ann and I both sat at the feet of elder Kathleen *Kemarre* Wallace who autobiographically captures the primacy of place more so than time:

> My birth certificate says 'Place of Birth: Unknown', but I know where I was born – I was born in front of the cave at Uyetye. We don't know exactly when I was born, but my mother and grandparents told me it was just before winter, when *Arralkwe*, the Seven Sisters, was just going down in the sky towards the horizon (Wallace, 2009, p. 55).

While Indigenous ways of life are commonly described as timeless, or beyond time, *Arrernte* elders from Central Australia such as Turner and Wallace challenge this idea. The well-known anthropologist W.E.H. Stanner suggested that 'abidingness' (which he defined as 'a very special value on things remaining unchangingly themselves') is more central than 'timelessness' (1987). This notion of abidingness is a fertile one for places called supervision. Drawing on the work of recently passed and respected lawman of the Dhurii clan of north-east Arnhem Land, Rev Dr Djiniyini Gondarra, Tony Swain documented how primacy of place, more so than time, is crucial in Indigenous perspectives (Swain, 1993). What if professional supervision for school leaders is primarily a *place* for reflexivity, rather a compartmentalised and commodified amount of *time* for reflection? For this to be meaningful, Swain's distinction between 'abiding events' and 'rhythmic events' requires a brief explanation. Challenging the use of 'dreamtime' (and, 'dreaming') as a simplified interpretation of *Jukurrpa* (Walpiri) or *Altjira* (Arrernte) from the central and western deserts of Australia, Swain writes that (ancestral) 'Abiding Events' are rather a realm, a location of source and energy (Swain, 1993, p. 33). *Kemarre* Wallace in her testimony earlier locates her birth in relation to the song(line)s of the Seven Sisters (*Arralkwe*), not to a specific month or year. Abiding events are co-joined, even coterminous with, the rhythmic events of everyday life. As important an implication for place is the shape of events. Place emerges, moves and establishes an abode. Sites have energy: intention, movement and abiding (Swain, 1993, p. 33). This written description – albeit by a non-Indigenous researcher – resonates with the first-hand testimony of the elders I (Geoff) walk with: places have energy, intention, and abidingness, not just people or recent events. What if the place called supervision learnt from these First Nations' perspectives, to become a place of energy, intention, movement, and abiding?

We respect (and have discovered) that some school leaders need time to recover the inner motivation of their work through remembering abiding events that are sources of their own knowledge, cultural wisdom, intention, and own movement. The busyness of school leadership and the incessant demands of its rhythms force most school leaders into thinking primarily about 'all that I need to do', rushing headstrong along time-bound linear trajectories for completion, solution, resolution. Questions of deeper coherence – and resonance – with the affective and effective flows of 'things to do' might generate a different conceptualisation of place and time.

Professional Supervision is an appropriate place to find and feel such resonance with a curiosity and unlearning with what it means to be present to the *place* of reflexivity rather than the *time*. Otherwise, in my (Geoff's) experience of more than a decade of supervising with senior leaders, fidelity to a calling (an abiding notion underlying vocation) is often displaced by the sheer effort required to get the job done.

Across various professions, burnout and resignation among leaders has become more frequent. Slowing down may help up to a point, but doing less work is often not an option. Supervision is a place where more enduring questions about *what is worth doing* are considered. It is created with conditions of resonance and attunement towards Rosa's 'rhythmic oscillation' such that interconnected flows within complex school environments can be realised.

CURA Presence in Supervision

What kind of presence is evoked in supervision – in these places of resonance and attunement? It remains true that the focus of supervision is on learning and professional practice. But it is the presence of mind of the supervisor and supervisee(s) in the room that makes this an embodied practice (even on zoom). Recently, Paterson conveyed the idea 'we don't take cases to supervision ... we *are* the case' (2019, p. 14), owing this insight to theologian John Patton (Patton, 2012). A simple application of this idea is the question, 'how will I show up?' 'How do I intend to be?'

In terms of the supervisor's role, Carroll famously quipped that 'I knew I wanted to become a spontaneous reflective supervisor by forgetting technique – but first I needed to learn the technique that I intend to forget' (Hewson & Carroll, 2016, p. 1). This reminds us that presence in supervision must always be accompanied by a theoretical framework, intention, and skill. Further, as Moore suggests, it relies on wearing your theory lightly but not going out without it (Moore, 2017). Showing up with presence, unencumbered by thoughts of other matters and without preoccupation with the models, theories, and anxieties of 'getting it right' or 'making it work' is important.

Attunement and resonance remain inextricably linked to the quality of presence in Professional Supervision. Moore counsels supervisees hoping to bring reflexive awareness to their work, to have 'an open mind and heart for empathic resonance' (Moore, 2017, p. 112). Empathic resonance is the emotional (rather than verbal) narrative which is attuned first to the supervisee's emotions, and then – in the case of group supervision – interacts through an emotional resonance with other group members. Attuned presence in supervision means noticing both 'familiar and unfamiliar emotions' and considering 'what might be communicated through the unfamiliar emotion' (Moore, 2017, p. 112). It would be a mistake, however, to think that attunement in supervision is merely emotional awareness and empathy. Moore's quote earlier about wearing theory lightly conveys the importance of working with a theoretical framework to guide practice. This supervisory attunement – which might be colloquially referred to as the work of the head and the heart – is what Moore refers to as 'thinking, feelingly' and 'feeling, thinkingly'. It is from these entanglements that new meaning and insights are made (Moore, 2017, p. 112). Attuning to oneself in supervising must be accompanied by attuning to the unseen (or, absent) others in a supervisee's storying. Attuning to those outside the place of supervision prepares the supervisee for how they can engage differently in their practice.

CURA Practices of Supervision

I (Geoff) am a keen kayaker and have been for a couple of decades. During COVID lockdowns, I discovered kayaking documentaries and one of my favourites is called River Runner (Sturgess, 2021) featuring Scott Lindgren. Scott became a world-class kayaker before the age of thirty but during a hiatus from the gruelling mental and physical demands of his chosen profession, he was diagnosed with a brain tumour. The documentary is a deeply human story, with some fantastic mountain and river scenery (making it perfect for lockdown bingeing). But it is also a surprisingly common story. Prior to his diagnosis, we see Scott finding success by avoiding weakness and vulnerability, using sheer force of will and unrelenting determination, becoming the best, only associating with a very small circle of the best kayakers, using addiction as the only way to relax, experiencing relationship disasters and so on. In the final scene, however, there is Scott's voiceover as he rides the biggest rapid of his life, thereby completing a lifelong dream of kayaking the four major Himalayan rivers. On this, he reflects:

> I tried to control everything in my life. Once I realized, with my tumor, that I had no control over that, I just surrendered to the flow of life. And I no longer try to control the outcome of anything. I just show up with my heart and it gave me so much freedom. (Sturgess, 2021)

Not being in control can be a fear of leaders and high achievers. Yet, resonant and attuned practices of Professional Supervision enable us to show up with our heart, adapt, and lean into the uncontrollability of school leadership, and find a deeper freedom. Here we draw on Rosa and describe them as: listening to ignite (Rosa's 'Being affected'); leaning into agency (Rosa's 'Self-efficacy'); learning reflexively (Rosa's 'Adaptive transformation'); and, leading in and through complexity (Rosa's 'Uncontrollability').

Listening to Ignite

In a reflexive place where the abiding and rhythmic events of school leadership can collide and converge, both supervisor and supervisee will be mutually affected if they are listening to ignite. This includes, yet goes beyond, emotional intelligence in that it is 'characterized by reciprocity and mutual transformation: the subject's experience of some other calling upon it which requires understanding or answering, but that also has the ability to change the subject' (Lijster, Celikates, & Rosa, 2019, p. 64). More simply, it is the call and response of genuine human interaction via the vital role of mirror neurons. Often working in and with high functioning teams in schools, principals can nevertheless experience isolation in leadership, demanding a lot of intuitive knowledge and experience. A growing consensus from scholars (Kahneman, 2011; Grant, 2021) speaks to the illusory nature of supposed expertise which is sometimes merely habit or overconfidence. Unless we can attune to our own inner life, Siegel argues that we can never successfully attune with another. Being affected, therefore, is vastly different to being alone – and listening to ignite, we suggest, bridges that divide in the life of school leaders. Being open to being vulnerable makes it possible to be affected by another (Brown, 2021), and is a foundational practice of supervision.

Leaning into Agency

The second practice enabling resonance and attunement in the supervision of school leaders is agency, also described as self-efficacy, and active response. This might appear obvious, yet we have lost count of the conversations with senior leaders across different professions who have lost a sense of their own agency, or sense of self-efficacy in their actions. Rosa's insight that control and self-efficacy are not the same is crucial for leaders working with and across complex, even uncontrollable, systems. Most policies and procedures in contemporary schooling, and the compliance and regulatory regimes attached to them appear as methods to tame the uncontrollable. There are, of course, policies and procedures that provide the necessary control for a range of non-negotiables such as having secure premises and procedures to make schools safe. But beyond that, schools remain assemblages of effective and affective flow. To cultivate self-efficacy in these flows, what if fidelity to profession (school leadership and/or teaching) served to support motivated and ethical actions beyond the reporting and compliance? Many leaders are drawn to education to serve and make a difference, beyond the baseline mandates to keep students safe and improving their test results. Enabling school leaders to make a real difference via their active engagement and understanding of how their actions influence and impact themselves and others in the assemblage of school life, defines this second, crucial practice of supervision.

Learning Reflexively

The third practice is the reflexive learning (referred to as 'adaptive transformation' by Rosa). Echoing philosopher Martin Buber's concept of *I-Thou*, Rosa believes 'when we resonate with the world, we are no longer the same afterwards. Experiencing resonance transforms us, and it is precisely this transformation that makes us feel alive' (Rosa, 2020, p. 34). His distinction between adaptive transformation and appropriation offers insight into the genuine exchange of supervisor and supervisee at the heart of supervision practice. Learning reflexively 'we must be open enough to be affected or changed, while at the same time we must be closed off enough to respond effectively with our own voice' (Rosa, 2020, p. 35). These are the 'mutually reinforcing outcomes' identified by Siegel who calls this 'adaptive self-regulation' (Siegel, 2007, p. 190). This is why reflexivity is fundamental in supervision and school leadership. The higher performance accelerated by good coaching does not require the same kind of reflexivity because excellence is more easily appropriated from one expert to another. In supervision practice, where the school leader always remains the expert, excellence cannot be divorced from fidelity. Resonance, according to Rosa, and attunement, according to Siegel, are grounded in trusting one's own ability to affect and be affected. It is the capacity for 'touching others and eliciting from them an accommodating response' (Rosa, 2020, p. 36). Coaching practices, emerging from the world of competitive sports and business, focus on achieving results. Supervision practices focus on learning reflexively and require resonance, something we associate more with the connective and affective worlds of creative expression and meaning-making.

Leading in and through Complexity

Resonance, by definition, cannot be manufactured or engineered by the will of the individual, no matter their expertise or excellence. Resonance can never be reduced to a method. We have been careful to use the language of finding (or fostering) resonance. For Rosa, 'resonance is inherently uncontrollable ... it is a peculiar characteristic of resonance that it can be neither forced nor prevented with absolute certainty' (Rosa, 2020, p. 36).

I [Geoff] am writing this paragraph in the afterglow of a poignant and powerful demonstration of professional supervision with a new cohort of school principals learning to become supervisors. The demonstration is not a role play – it's for real – and the supervisee (a principal recently completing the same training) brings a live topic. Over more than a decade, I have held these demonstrations countless times, knowing that what I am demonstrating cannot be reduced to a generalisable method. The uncontrollability of the live, unscripted and unrehearsed demonstration is conditional upon resonance and attunement. Novice supervisors in training are tempted to look at my skill and experience as a master craftsman of supervision practice. I invite them to look beyond method and technique to the dance of supervision instead.

Rosa notes 'the transformative effects of a resonant relationship always and inevitably elude any planning on the part of the subjects. They can neither be predicted nor controlled' (Rosa, 2020, p. 36). They are qualities that we have seen emerge in good supervision demonstrations. But this is too neat and we remain suspicious of attempts by writers to contain and control resonance and attunement with a formula. As Siegel more appropriately observes, 'attunement creates coherence in the mind':

> When we sense that resonance, when we become aware of being attuned we feel the state of our relational resonance. In this way, the resonance circuitry ... participates in creating a coherent state of mind. (Siegel, 2007, p. 169)

These four practices of resonance and attunement in supervision further resonate with my (Mary Ann's) colleagues' collaborative insights about unlearning. We saw these as practical principles to underpin reflective practice that seeks to invite curiosity and the potential for unlearning in complex contexts. These principles are aligned with what I now know and practise in Professional Supervision:

- to anticipate the discomfit of disruption
- to make small acts towards contexts that matter
- to shift attention to unlearning encounters
- to attune to the potential of the new
- to accept the ongoing mix of un/learning (Adapted from McLeod et al., 2020).

These explorations of CURA in the places, presence, and practices of supervision return us full circle in some ways to the purpose and intent of Professional Supervision, particularly for school leaders.

What happens when the group supervision of school leaders experiences a critical rupture? The school principal had announced her resignation almost a year in advance to allow for a smooth transition to a new principal. Two members of the executive seized the opportunity to take accrued long service leave for an entire school term. The principal then stepped aside from the group supervision for a period of time leaving younger, highly capable, yet less experienced, school leaders acting in senior roles of deputy principal. Each faced new challenges in these acting roles that were exciting and daunting. How would the group reflect together in the absence of the three, wise and experienced elders who were mentors and role models?

The roller coaster of emotions experienced by one school leader was demonstrated in my invitation that she physically move between two chairs. As she sat in one chair, she named the exciting highs of the new role ('deep down I know I've got this'). When she moved to the other chair the daunting lows were given voice ('everything has gone to shit'). In the acting principal role, she noticed how often she moved between these chairs each day. The other school leaders resonated with her experience and initially wondered if she needed their encouragement to sit in the chair called, 'I've got this'? She remained curious and would not permit this easy resolution to her roller-coaster of emotions in the new role. Attuned to her need to be able to confide in trusted colleagues when 'everything had gone to shit' she confidently asserted she needed permission to sit in the chair of lows, but not to remain there.

This school leader had moved beyond reflexive awareness *('my new role is a roller coaster of emotions') to a deeper,* critical reflexivity *('in this new role*

I need to be able to throw my hands up and vent to trusted colleagues'). Now she glimpsed the practical reflexivity *of doing it differently ('I must not remain in that chair too long in this acting role'). Her brave, honest and vulnerable reflections concluded with tears of a different kind: new and surprising tears. These tears were neither exasperation ('everything has gone to shit') nor exhilaration ('deep down I know I've got this') but an epiphany. This school leader was neither confined to one chair, nor the other, but had personal agency and professional encouragement from her colleagues to be in one chair, then the other, as the roller coaster of her new role unfolded.*

Perhaps it was the absence of the elders that enabled this deeper, nuanced reflection to occur? One observation seemed to confirm this. The three absent leaders, it was surmised, would each have insisted the young school leader, who they had mentored and nurtured, remain in the 'I've got this' chair, with their well-intentioned cheerleading, 'you've got this'. If present, the absent elders would eliminate the other chair. The gathered leaders, younger and less experienced than their elders, intuitively accepted the reality of both chairs, as the roller coaster of emerging school leadership. Courageous school leadership, it appeared, requires both resilience and reflexivity, determination and doubt.

The facilitator concluded by noticing that the leader had remained seated in the 'I've got this' chair for some time and imagined a future – perhaps in another decade – when she would be a school principal and not need the other chair. The radiant smile – through the tears – confirmed she already knew this to be true.

CURA Purpose of Supervision

Returning to the question of purpose – with the conditions of curiosity, unlearning, resonance, and attunement in play – here we reframe and distil our discussion in a series of question-making questions. We are experimenting with this set of questions as a practical scaffold to invite an application of our CURA musings to real contexts.

Each question, as consecutively ordered here, requires resonance and attunement to be honestly explored, as well as reserves for curiosity and unlearning. A discordant or rushed supervision will rarely progress beyond the initial question. Whereas a supervision with all conditions present will invite and enable quality practice and a sense of purpose and value. These are merely questions. They are not a script for practice, but an invitation to a creative and reflective flow of enquiry as we 'think with' the idea of supervision in education.

What Should I Do?

Encultured by school systems and the busyness of the everyday, educational leaders might be expected to usually begin their own reflective practice with the essential question: *what should I do*? While this might be a question of and for all novices in any professional context, it reappears in the demands and life cycles of school leadership. It is a forceful question in the assemblage of complex systems and competing priorities that vie for attention in a typical school day. In situations where it is impossible to do everything, the question launches curiosity – and is essential to bringing the other conditions into play.

What Enables Me to Do It Well?

Second is a question on effectiveness: *what enables me to do it well?* The desire for effectiveness and quality is a common trait among leaders, and a range of strategies may come to light in supervision conversations. Coaching, consultancy, more structured professional learning, and peer communities of practice are all ways to find and assess effective quality strategies. But this can also limit thinking to instrumental aims and impacts. So, let's lean in on the 'enabling' part of this question instead: How am I/my colleagues/the system being resourced and also resourcing others to 'do it well'? Supervision then becomes attuned to recognising and realising agency and self-efficacy in knowing what to do, and how to do it well.

What Do I Really Want to Do?

Third is a more existential reflection: *what do I really want to do*? Most honest school leaders, at the end of a tough week or exhausting term, will find themselves contemplating, 'is this what I really want to do?' It can activate generative questions about vocation that we ignore at our peril. It is also an introspective question about what we value. The purpose of supervision is to become curious and find resonance with inner knowing. Coupled with this, is the potential for unlearning what you thought you believed or most wanted to be true.

What Is Worth Doing?

Which leads us to the fourth and most enduring question, which is rarely asked. *What is worth doing?* Over-busy and over-committed leaders are more willing to begin with a slightly different ask: *what is* not *worth doing?* There is usually a long list of responsibilities that, with a moment's pause, reveals a litany of 'tasks I wished weren't mine'. Sometimes leaders need gentle reminding that the question is actually '*what* is *worth doing*'? A number of leaders we deeply admire fall silent at the question. Others respond quietly 'no-one has ever asked me that question'. The most surprising and revealing response was from an experienced school leader: 'I have been waiting ten years to have this conversation'.

While the intention of supervision may be to explore all four questions, our abiding movement is always oriented towards the fourth. Here is the place to resonate and attune to what really matters. It's the place where curiosity and unlearning come to fruition in wise action.

5 Closing

The significance of being reflexive, rather than merely doing reflection, emerged as a key insight as we co-authored this text. Being reflexive is essential but not necessarily easy for school leaders. Becoming reflexive may be relatively easeful to write about but, as we close this primer, it is essential that we attempt to write reflexively about our practice ourselves. How were we being affected through engaging with school leaders through supervision, through co-facilitating professional learning in supervision, and through writing this Element?

I (Geoff) spent most of yesterday with school leaders, reminded again of the challenges, complexities, and uncontrollability of school assemblages. Last night I heard myself say out loud 'I couldn't be a school principal'. This is not a flippant comment but a reflection of the descending heaviness I felt at the end of a long day. The day began in supervision with the head of a private school who was feeling the weight of public attention on all school leaders that inevitably follows media investigations of wrongdoing by others. Then I sat with the principal of a large public secondary school where I foolishly colluded in their joke about how easy it would be to be a primary school principal. The very next supervision session was with the principal of one of the larger primary schools in the State, where I had to confess (without disclosing details of course) of my earlier joking, as I felt the weight of responsibility on this primary principal's shoulders, which was surely no laughing matter. The day finished with the particular challenges of another principal in a school with a rapidly growing and diverse population in a region struggling economically and socially. My words, 'I couldn't be a school principal' came from a deep sense of admiration for the grit, grace, and passion of the school leaders I had spent the day with. I know that if we spent time with the other school leaders who might read this primer, we would be bearing witness to the same qualities of grit, grace, and passion. (If this is you, thank you for what you do.)

Each of the leaders that day exhibited the four conditions of CURA: self-curiosity ('am I showing up as I intend to be?'); the willingness to unlearn ('I don't have to control or fix everything and everyone' is a common unlearning);

finding resonance (as an alternative to acceleration and alienation); and being attuned (particularly attuned to one's own 'soul' in the work as well as the needs of others). Each of yesterday's school leaders was bearing a load. The act of sharing that load in a supervisory alliance – or partnership – lightened the burden, even if temporarily. In one instance, the principal was also able to share the load with the other senior leaders in their school team and sent through the following message after our session: 'Thank you. Today in exec we all shared what self care looks like'. Our primer on Professional Supervision for school leaders advocates for such load-sharing conversations as a crucial antidote to what is sometimes described by the principals we've worked with as a kind of isolation, even with brilliant teams by their sides.

We, as supervisors, share the privilege of bearing witness to school leaders' commitment, determination, and perseverance on behalf of their students and communities. The sustainable wellbeing of school leaders must remain a key priority for resourcing education and the systemic changes required. Professional Supervision, however, is not merely about support and wellbeing. Being reflexive invites more difficult questions on the other side of isolation and loneliness in principalship. Effective leadership in complex organisations demands professionals who are highly skilled, capable, and responsible. However, many leaders, regardless of their profession or discipline, can become confined by their expertise. The skills and abilities that helped them ascend to senior positions don't always translate seamlessly to the demands of leadership.

Yesterday, as each school leader leaned into the collaboration of the supervision session, they were awakened to the seductive myths of their professional role. These myths had been internalised: 'I, alone, can fix this'; 'I, alone, am capable'; and 'I, alone, am responsible'. Each of the school leaders I (Geoff) talked with that day were burdened with the weight of these (impossible) demands as well as the weight of the expectations of the role. The self-expectations and isolation had become entangled in a vicious cycle that was unmasked by my simple question to the principal who had sent a deputy home (for a mental health day) for the deputy's own wellbeing. I inquired, 'who gets to tell you to go home?' (The real possibility that this school leader might walk away from the role due to its demands had already emerged as a key focus of our supervision conversation). We paused to allow the obvious answer to my question sink in ('no-one'). Eventually I asked if we could re-negotiate our working agreement: that I might be one person the principal could allow to 'send them home'. This request could be made because a degree of empathetic resonance and emotional attunement was already evident in the supervision relationship. Agreement was reached and there was palpable relief on the principal's face: 'I am less alone and not solely responsible [for my own wellbeing]'.

The ethical dimension to being reflexive (or, leaning into moral purpose) is easily co-opted by regulation and compliance and becomes something done to, rather than done with, another person. Reflexively, I acknowledge that my background in the Anglican Church and academic theology brings with it a long and chequered history of heavy-handed (even abusive) enforcement of morality and ethics. Perhaps most large institutions resort to enforcing compliance instead of enabling fidelity to role? In supervision, however, the school leader was empowered – had regained a sense of agency and efficacy – by inviting a trusted supervisor to share responsibility for their wellbeing. My experience with senior leaders suggests that the result of this sharing means it is far less likely I'll ever have to 'send this principal home' from school (although the inner adolescent in me may regret writing this conclusion). 'I couldn't be a school principal' was an honest reflection of both my awe for those I had been with throughout the day and a deeper ache as I bore witness to what they carried, often alone.

*

It was the second week in the new school year for Lee. She'd decided to zoom in from home a little later than usual rather than pressure herself with thoughts of tackling the traffic home. It meant I (Mary Ann) got to (virtually) meet her dog. I smiled at the nuance behind Lee's initial insistence that she wasn't 'the fluffy type' – when her four-legged kin most definitely was.

Lee wanted to talk about the plans for the year, and the increasing commitment to the school vision among her staff to whom she was clearly very dedicated. She spoke in glowing terms about the children and families, praising their resilience. She acknowledged her tough love in keeping learning expectations high, especially since the students she most frequently encountered in her office were those facing devastating challenges or just 'in trouble'.

The vision she shared for the year was strong, so I asked what's on the mid-horizon – what did she want to be seeing and experiencing by the end of Term 2? I was taken by the vibrancy in her voice and the lightness of being she brought to her description.

'Ah, Lee, there's so much clarity in that. I'm imagining I'm standing on that horizon now and looking back at the landscape you've had to traverse to get here. I wonder if you were to look back from this horizon too – what advice would you give yourself? What would you want to say back to the principal sitting here, Week 2, Term 1?'

Lee's overarching vision for herself as a leader, shared when we first began supervision, was to be 'visionary, courageous, and passionate'. We'd been meeting regularly over the past year, which had been an immensely difficult one for the school community on so many counts.

> *'Advice? Ok. Be kind.'*
> *'What else?' I asked. A pause. She looked at me under her brow, thinking wasn't that enough?*
> *'Hmmm. Back yourself,' she responded.*
> *'Let's see if we can make it to three. What are three things you want to tell Lee sitting here with the fluffy beast of a dog sitting on her lap, at the beginning of Term 1?'*
> *Lee fake-grumbled, remembering that, yes, we do work hard together in this supervision thing. She takes a long breath.*
> *'Take the good in.'*
> *A moment. We sat in a slightly stunned, companionable silence. Both a little in awe of what she'd just uttered. It was so wise. It was something that Lee very rarely permitted herself to do.*

There's nothing more affecting as a supervisor, than to experience a genuine co-learning with another. Something that resonates in and beyond the moment. It's humbling to hold that moment for another person. It's also a privilege and a responsibility – not just for moments like these, but for the moments of discomfit and unlearning and reorientation which can feel so shaky and uncertain. My gratitude for my own supervisor looms large. Her capacity to do the same for me – to hold a moment to help reveal insight, be it a tough one, a wise one, a celebratory one, or an 'I just don't know' one – is integral to my own ongoing professional practice and learning, It reminds me of the saying 'it takes a village' when I think of us all walking alongside each other in this education gig.

> *'That sounds like really valuable advice. I wonder if you could say those three things again, so you can really hear them.'*
> *'Lee, back yourself.*
> *Lee, be kind.*
> *Lee, take it in.'*
> *Another moment. We didn't need any words after that. We smiled. I think we beamed. I think the fluff-dog beamed also. There may have been a shared tear or two.*
> *'Till next time' and we closed the zoom.*

*

What is really worth doing? We share a growing sense of purpose to make a difference for school leaders. It began with some small experiments in supervising school leaders and training principals to supervise others. We were caught by surprise by the enthusiasm generated as a response. Collectively, the grit and grace of the 30+ principals we've now worked with so far inspired us to write this primer. Now we arrive here ourselves, reflexive but attuned to the potential of Professional Supervision for school leaders. A journey together begun in curiosity, with lots of unlearning, buoyed and sustained by experience, and the process of finding resonance with each other and those we've shared ideas with along the way. We reached some outer edges of our own learning and are grateful for the dozens of colleagues who have joined us in conversation and practice on this. We are now also grateful for you, a wider circle of readers who have remained curious until the final page and encourage you to embark on further exploration of Professional Supervision for school leaders. That, we firmly believe, is worth doing.

References

Anderson, E. & Weiner, J. (2023). Managing up, down and outwards: Principals as boundary spanners during COVID 19 crisis. *School Leadership & Management*, 43(4), 1–19. https://doi.org/10.1080/13632434.2023.2171006.

Andrews, J. & Munro, C. (2018). Coaching for agency. In D. M. Netolicky, J. Andrews, & C. Paterson, eds., *Flip the System Australia: What Matters in Education*. London: Routledge, pp. 163–71. https://doi.org/10.4324/9780429429620.

Baglow, L. (2009). Social work supervision and its role in enabling a community visitor program that promotes and protects the rights of children. *Australian Social Work*, 62(3), 353–68.

Bainbridge, A., Reid, H., & Del Negro, G. (2022). Towards a virtuosity of school leadership: Clinical support and supervision as professional learning. *Professional Development in Education*, 48(4), 546–58. https://doi.org/10.1080/19415257.2019.1700152.

Bandura, A. (2012). On the functional properties of perceived self-efficacy revisited. *Journal of Management*, 38(1), 9–44.

Bates, A. & Burbank, M. (2019). *Agency in Teacher Supervision and Mentoring: Reinvigorating the Practice*. New York: Routledge.

Bawany S. (2016). NextGen leaders for a VUCA world. *Leadership Excellence Essentials*, 33(8), 43–44.

Baxter, L. P., Southall, A. E., & Gardner, F. (2021). Trialling critical reflection in education: The benefits for school leaders and teachers. *Reflective Practice*, 22(4), 501–51. https://doi.org/10.1080/14623943.2021.1927694.

Beddoe, L. (2010). Surveillance or reflection: Professional supervision in 'the risk society'. *British Journal of Social Work*, 40, 1279–96.

Beddoe, L. (2016). *Challenges in Professional Supervision*. London: Jessica Kingsley Publishers.

Bennett N. & Lemoine G. J. (2014 January–February). What VUCA really means for you. *Harvard Business Review*. https://hbr.org/2014/01/what-vuca-really-means-for-you.

Berlyne, D. E. (1954). A theory of human curiosity. *British Journal of Psychology*, 45, 180–91. http://dx.doi.org/10.1111/j.2044-8295.1954.tb01243.x.

Berlyne, D. E. (1960). *Conflict, Arousal and Curiosity*. New York: McGraw Hill.

Biesta, G. J. J. (2012). Giving teaching back to education: Responding to the disappearance of the teacher. *Phenomology & Practice*, 6(2), 35–49.

Biesta, G. J. J. (2013). *The Beautiful Risk of Education*. London: Routledge.

Biesta, G. & Tedder, M. (2007). Agency and learning in the lifecourse: Towards an ecological perspective. *Studies in the Education of Adults*, 39(2), 132–49.

Billet, S. & Newton, J. (2010). A learning practice: Conceptualising professional lifelong learning for the healthcare sector. In H. Bradbury, N. Frost, S. Kilminster, & M. Zukas, eds., *Beyond Reflective Practice: New Approaches to Professional Lifelong Learning*. London: Routledge, pp. 52–65.

Bogart, A. (2021). *The Art of Resonance*. London: Methuen Drama.

Brookfield, S. (2016). So what exactly is critical about critical reflection? In J. Fook, V. Collington, F. Ross, G. Ruch, & L. West, eds., *Researching Critical Reflection: Multidisciplinary Perspectives*. London: Routledge, pp. 11–22.

Broughton, G. (2021). *A Practical Christology for Pastoral Supervision*. Abingdon: Routledge.

Broughton, G., ed. (2024). *Look Again, Live Again: Supervision across the Pastoral Disciplines*. Sydney: Institute for Pastoral Supervision and Reflective Practice.

Brown, A. M. (2017). *Emergent Strategy: Shaping Change, Changing Worlds*. Chico, CA: AK Press.

Brown, B. (2021). *Atlas of the Heart: Mapping Meaningful Connection and the Language of Human Experience*. New York: Random House.

Brown, B., Wang, T., Lee, M., & Childs, A. (2023). Surviving, navigating and innovating through a pandemic: A review of research on school leadership during COVID 19, 2020–2021. *International Journal of Educational Development*, 100, 1–10. https://doi.org/10.1016/j.ijedudev.2023.102804.

Campbell, P., Hollweck, T., & Netolicky, D. M. (2023). Grappling with pracademia in education: Forms, functions, and futures. In Dickinson, J. & Griffiths, T. L., eds., *Professional Development for Practitioners in Academia: Knowledge Studies in Higher Education*. Cham: Springer, p. 13. https://doi.org/10.1007/978-3-031-33746-8_6.

Carroll, M. (2014). *Effective Supervision for the Helping Professions*. New York: Sage.

Carroll, M. (2011). Supervision: A journey of lifelong learning. In R. Shohet, ed., *Supervision as Transformation: A Passion for Learning*. London: Jessica Kingsley, pp. 14–28.

Carroll, M. & Gilbert, M. (2011). *On Being a Supervisee: Creating Learning Partnerships*. London: Vukani.

Cary, L. J. (2023). Messy leadership: Interrupting marketplace responses to leadership in learning and teaching. *Journal of School Leadership*, 33(2), 198–213. https://doi.org/10.1177/10526846221148633.

Chen-Levi, T., Buskila, Y., & Schechter, C. (2024). Leadership as agency. *International Journal of Educational Reform*, 33(2), 127–41.

Chrulew, M. & de Vos, R. (2019). Stories of unravelling and reworlding. *Cultural Studies Review*, 25(1), 23–28. https://doi.org/10.3316/informit.730865368982562.

Commonwealth of Australia. (2017). *Royal Commission into Institutional Responses to Child Sexual Abuse Final Report*. Canberra: Attorney-General's Department.

Cornforth, S. & Claiborne, L. B. (2008). When educational supervision meets clinical supervision: What can we learn from the discrepancies? *British Journal of Guidance and Counselling*, 36(2), 155–63.

Cunningham, C. (2019). An investigation into school inspection policies in Western Australian state education performed by the expert review group. *Educational Research for Policy and Practice*, 18, 39–58. https://doi.org/10.1007/s10671-018-9227-5.

Da-as, R., Oadach, M., & Schechter, C. (2023). Crisis leadership: Principals' metaphors during COVID 19. *Educational Management Administration & Leadership*. First published online April 20, 2023 [online]. https://doi.org/10.1177/17411432231170580.

Dadvand, B. (2022). Why restoring trust in teaching now could fix the teacher shortage. *EduResearch Matters*. September 12. www.aare.edu.au/blog/?p=14283.

Davys, A. & Beddoe, L. (2020). *Best Practice in Professional Supervision*. 2nd ed. Warriewood: Jessica Kingsley.

Deleuze, G. & Guattari. F. (1988). *A Thousand Plateaus: Capitalism and Schizophrenia*, trans. Brian Massumi. London: Athlone.

Dewey, J. (1925). *Experience and Nature*. Chicago, IL: Dover.

Dōgen, E. (2007). *Shōbōgenzō: The Treasure House of the Eye of the True Teaching*. California: Shasta Abbey Press.

Elliot, K. & Hollingsworth, H. (2020). *A Case for Reimagining School Leadership Development to Enhance Collective Efficacy*. Camberwell: Australian Council of Educational Research.

Escobar, A. (2020). *Pluriversal Politics: The Real and the Possible*. Durham, NC: Duke University Press.

Ewing, R., Waugh, F., & Smith, D. L. (2022). Introduction: What is reflection and reflective professional practice? In R. Ewing, F. Waugh, & D. L. Smith, eds., *Reflective Practice in Education and Social Work: Interdisciplinary Explorations*. Abingdon: Routledge, pp. 135–49.

Finnegan, J. (2010). Dialogue and theory in clinical supervision. In M. Benefiel & G. Holton, eds., *The Soul of Supervision: Integrating Practice and Theory*. New York: Morehouse, pp. 120–51.

Flessner, R., Miller, G. R., Patrizio, K. M., & Horwitz, J. R. (2012). *Agency Through Teacher Education: Reflection, Community, and Learning*. New York: Rowman & Littlefield Education.

Fowlie, H. (2016). Relational supervision — A two-person approach. In H. Hargaden, ed., *The Art of Relational Supervision: Clinical Implications of the Use of Self in Group Supervision*. London: Routledge, pp. 45–61.

Garver, R. (2020). Evaluative relationships: Teacher accountability and professional culture. *Journal of Education Policy*, 35(5), 623–47. https://doi.org/10.1080/02680939.2019.1566972.

Glanz, J. (2022). Personal reflections on supervision as instructional leadership: From whence it came and to where shall it go? *Journal of Educational Supervision*, 4(3) [online]. https://doi.org/10.31045/jes.4.3.5.

Gorrell, A. & De Nobile, J. (2023). The well-being of Australian primary school principals: A study of the key concerns. *International Journal of Educational Management*, 37(6/7), 1243–54. https://doi.org/10.1108/IJEM-01-2023-0039.

Grant, A. M. (2021). *Think Again: The Power of Knowing What You Don't Know*. New York: Viking.

Grisold, T. & Kaiser, A. (2017). Leaving behind what we are not: Applying a systems thinking perspective to present unlearning as an enabler for finding the best version of the self. *Journal of Organisational Transformation & Social Change*, 14(1), 39–55.

Groundwater-Smith, S. (2022). Conversation and the reflexive turn in social practice. In R. Ewing, F. Waugh, & D. L. Smith, eds., *Reflective Practice in Education and Social Work: Interdisciplinary Explorations*. Abingdon: Routledge, pp. 135–49.

Gupta, D., Boland, R., & Aron, D. (2017). The physician's experience of changing clinical practice: A struggle to unlearn. *Implementation Science*, 12(28), 1–11.

Hawkins, P. (1985). Humanistic psychotherapy supervision: A conceptual framework. *Self & Society*, 13(2), 69–76.

Hawkins, P. (2011). Systemic coaching supervision. In T. Bachkirova, P. Jackson, & D. Clutterbuck, eds., *Supervision in Mentoring and Coaching: Theory and Practice*. Maidenhead: Open University Press, pp. 167–82.

Hawkins, P. & McMahon, A. (2020). *Supervision in the Helping Professions*. 5th ed. Maidenhead: McGraw Hill Education.

Hawkins, P. & Shohet, R. (2006). *Supervision in the Helping Professions*. Maidenhead: Open University Press.

Heifetz, R. A., Grashow, A., & Linsky, M. (2009). *The Practice of Adaptive Leadership: Tools and Tactics for Changing Your Organization and the World*. Boston, MA: Harvard Business Press.

Hewson, D. & Carroll, M. (2016). *Reflective Practice in Supervision*. Hazelbrook: Moshpit.

Holloway, J. (2021). *Metrics, Standards and Alignment in Teacher Policy: Critiquing Fundamentalism and Imagining Pluralism*. Singapore: Springer.

Johns, C. (2001). Depending on the intent and emphasis of the supervisor, clinical supervision can be a different experience. *Journal of Nursing Management*, 9(3), 139–45.

Kahneman, D. (2011). *Thinking, Fast and Slow*. London: Allen Lane.

Kaldor, P., Nash, N., & Paterson, S. E. (2017). *Rethinking Leadership: Building Capacity for Positive Change*. Sydney: Thousand Lakes.

Karvinen-Niinikoski, S., Beddoe, L., Ruch, G., & Tsui, M. (2017). *Professional Supervision and Professional Autonomy*. Bristol: Policy Press.

Kemmis, S. (2005). Knowing practice: Searching for saliences. *Pedagogy, Culture & Society*, 13(3), 391–426. https://doi.org/10.1080/14681360500200235.

Kidson, P. (2023). *Interim Evaluation Report. Reflective Supervision in Education: Professional Learning for Facilitators*. Sydney: Kidson Educational Consulting.

Kidson, P. (2024). *Final Evaluation Report. Reflective Supervision in Education: Professional Learning for Facilitators*. Sydney: Kidson Educational Consulting.

Kline, N. (1999). *Time to Think: Listening to Ignite the Human Mind*. London: Cassell.

Langer, E. (1989). *Mindfulness*. Cambridge, MA: Perseus.

Larsen, E., Jensen-Clayton, C., Curtis, E., Loughland, T., & Nguyen, T. M. Hoa (2023). Re-Imagining teacher mentoring for the future. *Professional Development in Education* [online]. https://doi.org/10.1080/19415257.2023.2178480.

Leach, J. & Paterson, M. (2015). *Pastoral Supervision: A Handbook*. London: SCM.

Levitin, D. J. (2014). *The Organised Mind: Thinking Straight in the Age of Information Overload*. New York: Plume.

Lijster, T., Celikates, R., & Rosa, H. (2019). Beyond the echo-chamber: An interview with Hartmut Rosa on resonance and alienation. *Krisis*, 39(1), 64–78.

Long, J. S., McKenzie-Robblee, S., Schaefer, L., et al. (2012). Literature review on induction and mentoring related to early career teacher attrition and retention. *Mentoring and Tutoring: Partnership in Learning*, 20(1), 7–26, https://doi.org/10.1080/13611267.2012.645598.

Macy, J. (2021). *World as Lover, World as Self: Courage for Global Justice and Planetary Awakening*. 30th Anniversary Edition. Berkeley, CA: Parallax Press.

Mason, B. (2022). Towards positions of safe uncertainty. *Human Systems: Therapy, Culture and Attachments*, 2(2), 54–63.

McLeod K., Thakchoe, S., Hunter, M., et al. (2020). Principles for a pedagogy of unlearning. *Reflective Practice*, 21(2), 183–97. https://doi.org/10.1080/14623943.2020.173078.

Macdonald, G. (2002). Transformative unlearning: Safety, discernment and communities of learning. *Nursing Inquiry*, 9(3), 170–78.

McNary, L. (2023). Curiosity: A conceptual re-analysis for improved measurement. *Current Pscyhology*, 43(1), 1–12. https://doi.org/10.1007/s12144-022-04170-z.

McNiff, J. (2013). *Action Research: Principles and Practice*, 3rd ed. London: Routledge.

McWilliam, E. (2008). Unlearning how to teach. *Innovations in Education and Teaching International*, 45(3), 263–69.

Mezirow, J. (1990). *Fostering Critical Reflection in Adulthood: A Guide to Transformative and Emancipatory Learning*. San Francisco, CA: Jossey-Bass.

Millar, N. R. (2018). *Up Close and Professional: Integrative Reflection in Theory and in Practice*. Unpublished PhD Dissertation, University of Canberra.

Moore, B. (2017). *Reflexive Supervision: A Workbook for Learning within and across Professions*. Self-published, CreateSpace Independent Publishing Platform.

Moore, R. M. (2010). A process framework for learning in a new era of supervision. In M. Benefiel, M. & Holton, G., eds., *The Soul of Supervision: Integrating Practice and Theory*. New York: Morehouse, pp. 166–86.

Netolicky, D. M. (2020). School leadership during a pandemic: navigating tensions. *Journal of Professional Capital & Community*, 5(3/4), 391–95.

Nicolini, D. (2013). *Practice Theory, Work, and Organization: An Introduction*. Oxfordshire: Oxford University Press.

Northcott, N. (2000). Clinical supervision: Professional development or management control. In J. Spouse & L. Redfern, eds., *Successful Supervision in Health Care Practice*. London: Blackwell Science, pp. 10–29.

Panthalookaran, V. (2022). Education in a VUCA-driven world: Salient features of an entrepreneurial pedagogy. *Higher Education for the Future*, 9(2), 234–49. https://doi.org/10.1177/23476311221108808.

Palmer, P. J. (2004). Across the great divide: Rejoining soul and role. In P. J. Palmer, *A Hidden Wholeness: The Journey Toward an Undivided Life: Welcoming the Soul and Weaving Community in a Wounded World*. San Francisco, CA: Jossey-Bass, pp. 13–29.

Paterson, M. (2019). Discipled by praxis: Soul and role in context. *Practical Theology*, 12(1), 7–19.

Patton, J. (2012). Embodying Wisdom: Pastoral Proverbs for Reflective Practice. *Reflective Practice: Formation and Supervision in Ministry*, 32, 132–42.

Polanyi, M. (2009). *The Tacit Dimension*. Chicago, IL: University of Chicago Press.

Perryman, J. & Calvert, G. (2020). What motivates people to teach, and why do they leave? Accountability, performativity and teacher retention. *British Journal of Educational Studies*, 68(1), 3–23. https://doi.org/10.1080/00071005.2019.1589417.

Reid, H. & Soan, S. (2018). Providing support to senior managers in schools via 'clinical' supervision: A restorative and purposeful professional and personal space. *Professional Development in Education*, 45(1), 59–72. https://doi.org/10.1080/19415257.2018.1427132.

Reio, T. G., Jr., Petrosko, J. M., Wiswell, A. K., & Thongsukmag, J. (2006). The measurement and conceptualisation of curiosity. *The Journal of Genetic Psychology: Research and Theory on Human Development*, 167(2), 117–35. http://dx.doi.org/10.3200/GNTP.167.2.117-135.

Rosa, H. (2019). *Resonance: A Sociology of The Relationship to the World*. Medford, MA: Polity Press.

Rosa, H. (2020). *The Uncontrollability of the World*. Cambridge: Polity Press.

Ryan, R. M. & Deci, E. L. (2017). *Self-determination Theory: Basic Psychological Needs in Motivation, Development, and Wellness*. New York: The Guilford Press. https://doi.org/10.1521/978.14625/28806.

Ryan, S. (2004). *Vital Practice: Stories from the Healing Arts – The Homeopathic and Supervisory Way*. Bexhill on Sea: Sea Change Publications.

Safe Work Australia. (2023). *Model Work Health and Safety Regulations*. Canberra: Parliamentary Counsel's Committee. www.safeworkaustralia.gov.au/sites/default/files/2023-08/model-whs-regulations-1_august_2023.pdf.

Sahlberg, P. (2016). The global education reform movement and its impact on schooling. In K. Mundy, A. Green, B. Lingard, & A. Verger, eds., *The Handbook of Global Education Policy*. New Jersey: John Wiley & Sons, pp. 128–44.

Scaife, J. (2010). *Supervising the Reflective Practitioner: An Essential Guide to Theory and Practice*. London: Routledge.

Schön, D. A. (1984). *The Reflective Practitioner: How Professionals Think in Action*. London: Routledge.

See, S. M., Kidson, P., Dicke, T., & Marsh, H. (2023). *The Australian Principal Occupational Health, Safety and Wellbeing Survey (IPPE Report): 2022 Data*. Sydney: Institute for Positive Psychology and Education, Australian Catholic University.

Sergiovanni, T. J., Rubin, L. J., Manolakes, T. & House, E. R. (1975). *Professional Supervision for Professional Teachers*. Washington, DC: Association for Supervision and Curriculum Development.

Siegel, D. J. (2007). *The Mindful Brain: Reflection and Attunement in the Cultivation of Well-Being*. New York: W. W. Norton.

Stanner, W. E. H. (1987). The dreaming. In W. H. Edwards, ed., *Traditional Aboriginal Society: A Reader*. South Melbourne: Macmillan, pp. 220–37.

Strom, K., Haas, E., Danzig, A., Martinez, E., & McConnell, K. (2018). Preparing educational leaders to think differently in polarized, post-truth times. *The Educational Forum*, 82(3), 259–77.

Sturgess, R. (2021). *The River Runner*. USA, Netflix: 86 mins.

Swain, T. (1993). *A Place for Strangers: Towards a History of Australian Aboriginal Being*. Cambridge: Cambridge University Press.

Taguma, M. & Gabriel, F. (2018). Preparing humanity for change and artificial intelligence: Learning to learn as a safeguard against volatility, uncertainty, complexity and ambiguity. *Future of Education and Skills 2030*: Curriculum Analysis. Report of the 8th Informal Working Group (IWG) Meeting. Paris. www.oecd.org/education/2030/Preparing-humanity-for-change-and-artificial-intelligence.pdf.

Thompson, C. (2022). *Reflective Practice for Professional Development: A Guide for Teachers*. Abingdon: Routledge.

Thomson, P. & Greany, T. (2024). The best of times, the worst of times: Continuities in school leaders' work in uncertain times. *Educational Management Administration and Leadership* [online]. https://doi.org/10.1177/17411432231218544.

Tlostanova, M. & Mignolo, W. (2012). *Learning to Unlearn: Decolonial Reflections from Eurasia and the Americas*. Columbus, OH: The Ohio State University Press.

Torrance, D., Mifsud, D., Niesche, R., & Fertig, M. (2023). Headteachers and the pandemic: Themes from a review of literature on leadership for professional learning in complex times. *Professional Development in Education*, 49(6), 1103–16. https://doi.org/10.1080/19415257.2023.2229333.

Turner, M. K. (2010). *Iwenhe tyerrtye: What it means to be an Aboriginal person*, as told to Barry McDonald Perrurle, trans Veronic Perrurle Dobson. Alice Springs; IAD Press.

Van Nieuwerburgh, C., Barr, M., Munro C., Noon, H., & Arifin, D. (2020). Experiences of aspiring school principals receiving coaching as part of a leadership development programme. *International Journal of Mentoring and Coaching in Education*, 9(3), 291–306.

Vaughn, M., Wall, A., Scales, R., Parsons, S., & Sotirovska, V. (2021). Teaching visioning: A systematic review of the literature. *Teaching and Teacher Education*, 108(8), 1–11.

Wallace, K. (2009). *Listen Deeply: Let These Stories In*. Alice Springs: IAD Press.

Wheatley, M. J. & Frieze, D. (2018). *Walk Out Walk On: A Learning Journey into Communities Daring to Live the Future Now*. Melbourne: Penguin.

Zeichner, K. M. (2018). *The Struggle for the Soul of Teacher Education*. New York: Routledge. https://doi.org/10.4324/9781315098074.

Zepeda, S. J. (2016). *Instructional Supervision: Applying Tools and Concepts*, 4th ed. London: Routledge. https://doi.org/10.4324/9781315625874.

Zuss, M. (2011). *The Practice of Theoretical Curiosity: Explorations of Educational Purpose*. Dordrecht: Springer.

Cambridge Elements

Critical Issues in Teacher Education

Tony Loughland
University of New South Wales

Tony Loughland is an Associate Professor in the School of Education at the University of New South Wales, Australia. Tony is currently leading projects on using AI for citizens' informed participation in urban development, the provision of staffing for rural and remote areas in NSW and on Graduate Ready Schools.

Andy Gao
University of New South Wales

Andy Gao is a Professor in the School of Education at the University of New South Wales, Australia. He edits various internationally-renowned journals, such as International Review of Applied Linguistics in Language Teaching for De Gruyter and Asia Pacific Education Researcher for Springer.

Hoa T. M. Nguyen
University of New South Wales

Hoa T. M. Nguyen is an Associate Professor in the School of Education at the University of New South Wales, Australia. She specializes in teacher education/development, mentoring and sociocultural theory.

Editorial Board
Megan Blumenreich, *CUNY*
Ricardo Cuenca, *Universidad Nacional Mayor de San Marcos, Peru*
Viv Ellis, *Monash University*
Declan Fahie, *UCD Dublin*
Amanda Gutierrez, *ACU Australia*
Jo Lampert, *Monash University*
Lily Orland-Barak, *University of Haifa*
Auli Toom, *University of Helsinki*
Simone White, *RMIT Australia*
Juhan Ye, *BNU China*
Hongbiao Yin, *Chinese University of Hong Kong*
Zhu Xhudong, *BNU China*

About the Series
This series addresses the critical issues teacher educators and teachers are engaged with in the increasingly complex profession of teaching. These issues reside in teachers' response to broader social, cultural and political shifts and the need for teachers' professional education to equip them to teach culturally and linguistically diverse students.

Cambridge Elements ☰

Critical Issues in Teacher Education

Elements in the Series

Interculturality, Criticality and Reflexivity in Teacher Education
Fred Dervin

Enhancing Educators' Theoretical and Practical Understandings of Critical Literacy
Vera Sotirovska and Margaret Vaughn

Reclaiming the Cultural Politics of Teaching and Learning: Schooled in Punk
Greg Vass

Language Teacher's Social Cognition
Hao Xu

Who am I as a Teacher? Migrant Teachers' Redefined Professional Identity
Annika Käck

Professional Supervision for Principals: A Primer for Emerging Practice
Mary Ann Hunter and Geoff Broughton

A full series listing is available at: www.cambridge.org/EITE

For EU product safety concerns, contact us at Calle de José Abascal, 56–1°,
28003 Madrid, Spain or eugpsr@cambridge.org.

www.ingramcontent.com/pod-product-compliance
Ingram Content Group UK Ltd.
Pitfield, Milton Keynes, MK11 3LW, UK
UKHW020045160325
456256UK00019B/489